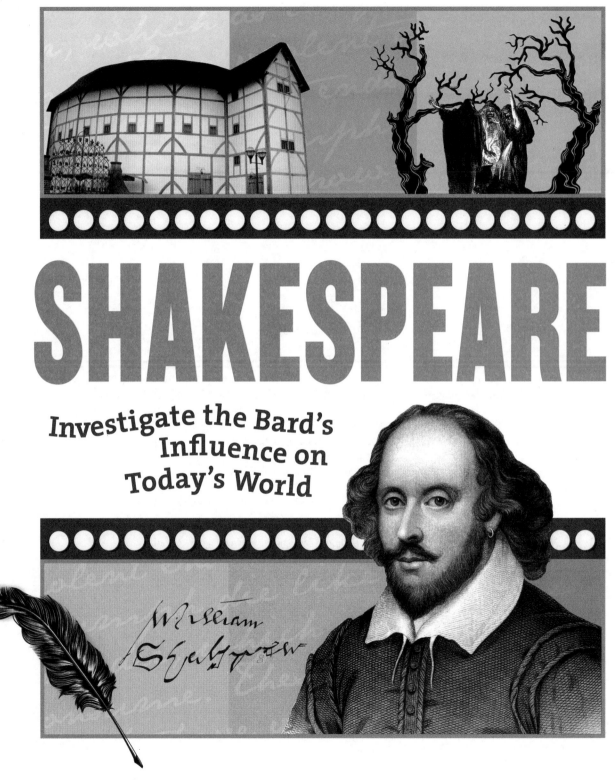

SHAKESPEARE

Investigate the Bard's Influence on Today's World

INQUIRE AND INVESTIGATE

Andi Diehn
Illustrated by Samuel Carbaugh

Nomad Press
A division of Nomad Communications
10 9 8 7 6 5 4 3 2 1

This book was manufactured by Marquis Book Printing,
Montmagny, Québec, Canada
November 2016, Job #125548
ISBN Softcover: 978-1-61930-455-0
ISBN Hardcover: 978-1-61930-451-2

Educational Consultant, Marla Conn

Questions regarding the ordering of this book should be addressed to
Nomad Press
2456 Christian St.
White River Junction, VT 05001
www.nomadpress.net

Printed in Canada.

Social Studies titles in the **Inquire and Investigate** series

Whether 'tis nobler in the mind to suffer
The slings and arrows of outrageous fortune,
Or to take arms against a sea of troubles
And by opposing end them. To die—to sleep,
No more; and by a sleep to say we end
The heart-ache and the thousand natural shocks
That flesh is heir to: 'tis a consummation
Devoutly to be wish'd. To die, to sleep;
To sleep, perchance to dream—ay, there's the rub
For in that sleep of death what dreams may come
When we have shuffled off this mortal coil,
Must give us pause—there's the respect
That makes calamity of so long life.
For who would bear the whips and scorns of
Th'oppressor's wrong, the proud man's contumely,
The pangs of dispriz'd love; the law's delay,
The insolence of office, and the spurns
That ...
Whe...
With...
To g...
But...

Interested in primary sources?

PS

Look for this icon.

You can use a smartphone or tablet app to scan the QR codes and explore more about Shakespeare! Cover up neighboring QR codes to make sure you're scanning the right one. You can find a list of URLs on the Resources page.

If the QR code doesn't work, try searching the Internet with the Keyword Prompts to find other helpful sources. 🔍 Shakespeare

Contents

TIMELINE

Scholars don't know the exact years Shakespeare wrote his plays, so the years have the word *circa*, or its abbreviation *c*, in front of them, which means "approximately."

1564............................ William Shakespeare is born in Stratford, England. His father, John, is a glover and is active in town politics. His mother gives birth to five more children after Shakespeare.

1582............................ Shakespeare marries Anne Hathaway. Anne is eight years older than Shakespeare.

1583............................ Susanna Shakespeare, their first child, is born.

1585............................ The twins, Judith and Hamnet, are born to Shakespeare and Anne.

1585–1592................ This span is known as the "lost years," because there is no documentation of Shakespeare's activities or whereabouts during this time. Theories about where he was include working in a law office and joining a battle.

circa 1590................ Shakespeare writes his first plays, including *The Comedy of Errors*, *The Two Gentleman of Verona*, *King John*, and *Henry VI, Part 1*.

c. 1591...................... Shakespeare writes *Henry VI, Part 2*.

1592.........................Robert Greene, a writer and critic, gives the first mention of Shakespeare as a writer: "There is an upstart crow, beautified with our feathers, that with his 'Tiger's heart wrapt in a player's hide' supposes he is well able to bombast out blank verse as the best of you: and … is in his own conceit the only Shake-scene in a country."

c. 1592.....................Shakespeare writes *Henry VI, Part 3*.

c. 1593.....................Shakespeare writes *Venus and Adonis* and *Richard III*.

1593–1594...............All London theaters are closed due to a plague outbreak.

c. 1594.....................Shakespeare writes *The Taming of the Shrew*, *Titus Andronicus*, *The Rape of Lucrece*, *Romeo and Juliet*, and *Love's Labours Lost*.

c. 1595.....................Shakespeare writes *Richard II* and *A Midsummer Night's Dream*.

1596.........................Shakespeare's son, Hamnet, dies at 11 years old. The location of his grave is unknown.

c. 1596.....................Shakespeare writes *The Merchant of Venice* and *Henry IV, Part 1*.

TIMELINE

1597..........................Shakespeare buys New Place in Stratford, a house on 107 acres, for the price of 320 pounds. His family lives there while he stays in London working much of the time.

c. 1597......................Shakespeare writes *Henry IV, Part 2* and *The Merry Wives of Windsor.*

c. 1598......................Shakespeare writes *Much Ado About Nothing.*

1599..........................The acting company that Shakespeare is a part of, Lord Chamberlain's Men, builds and opens the Globe Theatre. In 1613, the theater burns to the ground after the roof catches fire when a cannon is fired during Shakespeare's play, *Henry VIII.* It is rebuilt in 1614.

c. 1599......................Shakespeare writes *As You Like It, Julius Caesar,* and *Henry V.*

c. 1600......................Shakespeare writes *Hamlet* and *Troilus and Cressida.*

1601..........................Shakespeare's father dies.

c. 1601......................Shakespeare writes *Twelfth Night* and *All's Well That Ends Well.*

c. 1603........................Shakespeare writes *Othello* and *Measure for Measure*.

1603............................Queen Elizabeth dies and her distant cousin, King James, takes over the throne. Shakespeare's acting company is renamed the King's Men in honor of the new king. They perform for King James at least 11 times.

c. 1605........................Shakespeare writes *King Lear* and *Timon of Athens*.

c. 1606........................Shakespeare writes *Macbeth*.

c. 1607........................Shakespeare writes *Pericles* and *Antony and Cleopatra*.

1608............................Shakespeare's mother dies.

c. 1608........................Shakespeare writes *Coriolanus*.

1609............................A collection of Shakespeare's sonnets is published.

c. 1609........................Shakespeare writes *The Winter's Tale* and *Cymbeline*.

c. 1610........................Shakespeare writes *The Tempest*.

c. 1611........................Shakespeare writes *The Two Noble Kinsmen*.

c. 1613........................Shakespeare writes *Henry VIII*.

1616............................Shakespeare dies and is buried in Stratford. His tombstone reads:

Good friend for Jesus' sake forbeare,
To dig the dust enclosed here.
Blessed be the man that spares these stones,
And cursed be he that moves my bones.

1623............................The first collection of Shakespeare's plays is published by his friends, John Heminges and Henry Condell, in an edition known as the First Folio.

Shakespeare Past and Present

What influence does Shakespeare have on the books, movies, music, and poems of today?

Many contemporary works of art and literature refer to plots, characters, imagery, and language used by Shakespeare in the sixteenth century.

What does a writer who lived more than 400 years ago have to do with a movie you might watch on your laptop on a Saturday night? More than you think.

"I actually miss that stupid . . . I miss R! I know that's crazy, but is it really that crazy? Just because he's . . . whatever he is? I mean, isn't 'zombie' just a silly name we came up with for a state of being we don't understand? What's in a name, right?"

In the 2013 movie *Warm Bodies*, Julie is standing on the balcony of her father's house, lamenting the fact that the boy she likes, R, is a zombie. Because he's a zombie, her father disapproves of him and her friends don't really understand the relationship.

More than 400 years before Julie complained about her relationship problems on the big screen, audiences watched another girl, Juliet Capulet, struggle with the same dilemma. But Juliet wasn't in love with a zombie. She was in love with a boy named Romeo, who happened to be the son of the family her parents had been fighting with for many years.

For Juliet, falling in love with a member of the Montague family was one of the worst things that could happen to her. "Romeo, oh Romeo, wherefore art thou, Romeo?" she begins while standing on a balcony.

> 'Tis but thy name that is my enemy;
> Thou art thyself, though not a Montague.
> What's Montague? it is nor hand, nor foot,
> Nor arm, nor face, nor any other part
> Belonging to a man. O, be some other name!
> What's in a name? that which we call a rose
> By any other name would smell as sweet.
>
> (act 2 scene 2)

Julie and Juliet aren't real people. Julie is a character in a movie based on a book. Juliet is a character in a play by William Shakespeare written centuries ago. Is it a coincidence that they have similar names and similar problems? No. People have been using the plots, themes, characters, imagery, and language of Shakespeare since he first wrote and performed his plays in the late 1500s and early 1600s.

SHAKESPEARE'S EARLY YEARS

Because Shakespeare's work is very famous and still performed in theaters all around the world, it's natural to want to know about the man who wrote the plays and sonnets that hold audiences captive in their seats. Unfortunately, we don't know very much about Shakespeare. Even after many people have spent thousands of hours of effort trying to find out the details about his life, we know very little about him.

PRIMARY SOURCES

Primary sources come from people who were eyewitnesses to events. They might write about the event, take pictures, post short messages to social media or blogs, or record the event for radio or video. Why are primary sources important? Do you learn differently from primary sources than from secondary sources, which come from people who did not directly experience the event?

PS

Back in Shakespeare's time, many of the buildings were built out of wood and had thatched roofs of straw. Couple this with the fact that fire was used for heating and cooking, and you've got frequent tragedy. Many written records were lost when homes and businesses went up in flames.

[**The exact date of Shakespeare's birth is unknown.**]

We do know that Shakespeare was born in 1564 in a town called Stratford-upon-Avon. The town lies about 100 miles north of London, England, on the Avon River. While we don't know the date of his birth, we do know that Shakespeare was baptized on April 26, 1564. People generally agree that April 23 is Shakespeare's birthday. This is also the date of his death in 1616, 52 years later.

We know he was born to parents named John and Mary Shakespeare. John and Mary had eight children in all, four daughters and four sons. Not much is known about any of them, and at least two of them died in infancy. John was a glover and whitawer, or someone who works with soft leather. He also served in several municipal roles of increasing importance and authority.

These roles including constable, burgess, chamberlain, alderman, and finally, high bailiff, the highest elected position in town. This was similar to mayor. He was probably very well respected for a time. Later, though, he was involved in money-lending, an illegal practice, and he withdrew from the public eye.

A local grammar school called the King's New School welcomed boys aged seven and older. While no record exists of Shakespeare having attended the school, we assume he went until he was at least 12 years old.

During the 1500s, school was different from what it is today. Children arrived at six in the morning and stayed until five or six in the afternoon, sitting on hard wooden benches. They might only have two breaks during the entire day. Classes were held six days a week, year round. Children learned the alphabet by reading stories from the Bible and from collections of fables. They later learned Latin. As they grew older, students were forbidden to do any of their schoolwork in English or even speak it. Latin was the only language allowed in the schoolroom.

Shakespeare probably left school at about age 15, and at age 18 married a woman who was eight years older than him, Anne Hathaway. Very little is known about Anne apart from the fact that she died in 1623. She had three children with William Shakespeare—Susanna in May 1583 and twins Judith and Hamnet in February 1585.

The period of time from after the birth of the twins in 1585 up until 1592 are known as Shakespeare's "lost years." In 1592, there was a bitter mention of Shakespeare as an "upstart crow" from a writer named Robert Greene. But scholars have no idea what Shakespeare was up to. We know that at some point he left Stratford—and presumably his family—to go to London. He began writing plays and even performed in plays. We also know that his son, Hamnet, died in 1596. But there is no record of how Shakespeare felt about that or even if he attended the funeral.

VOCAB LAB

There is a lot of new vocabulary in this book! Turn to the glossary in the back when you come to a word you don't understand. Practice your new vocabulary in the **VOCAB LAB** activities in each chapter.

What happened in the years between Shakespeare's birth and death is one of the greatest literary mysteries of all time.

SHAKESPEARE ON STAGE

If you go to a theater today, you will probably sit on a plush seat in an enclosed space. On the stage ahead of you, lights will create different effects and a sound system will make it possible to hear everything the actors are saying. You'll be expected to remain quiet during the performance, which will last a couple of hours or so, and to be respectful of people sitting around you

In Shakespeare's time, theaters were much different. For one thing, it was open to the elements. No roof kept the rain or snow or wind out of the theater.

[
For a penny, people could stand in the area right in front of the stage to watch the show.
]

These spectators were called "groundlings." This was the cheapest spot to watch the play from, but it was also where the pickpockets hung out. For another penny, you could get a seat on a bench in one of the levels above. Royalty and nobility could pay more to sit fairly comfortably right up near the stage, or even on the stage itself.

Instead of quietly watching the performance, audiences in the Elizabethan Age jostled each other and ate snacks, including apples, pears, nuts, and gingerbread, and drank bottles of ale. There was little scenery and no curtains, so scene changes often had to rely on verbal cues from the actors.

Also, there were no female actors. All parts were played by men, which made plots about women posing as men and men posing as women even more confusing and funny.

Shakespeare was very successful as a playwright during his lifetime, though he might not have suspected he was to become one of the most important writers in English. Many of his plays were performed by his acting company, Lord Chamberlain's Men. In 1603, when Queen Elizabeth died, King James ascended the throne and took over patronage of the company, which then became known as the King's Men. Shakespeare owned a share of this company, which meant he was partly accountable for its debt and he also received a portion of the profits.

Lord Chamberlain's Men was the first acting company to build its own theater. When their lease on another London theater was not renewed, the actors tore the timber down and brought it across the river and built the Globe, which opened in 1599. Here they performed many of Shakespeare's greatest plays, including *Hamlet*, *Julius Caesar*, *Othello*, and *King Lear*.

Unfortunately, during a production of *Henry VIII* in 1613, a cannon misfired and ignited the building. The theater was rebuilt, but like all other theaters, it was shut down in 1642 by the Puritans. This powerful group of people believed theaters and plays were evil and one of the causes of moral indecency in society.

Shakespeare's plays were beloved by people all over England. He made enough money to purchase large tracts of land back in Stratford, where he seems to have visited fairly frequently.

FOLIO FACT

The Elizabethan Age was the period of time between 1558 and 1603 when Queen Elizabeth I ruled England. It's known as a golden age of prosperity, peace, and a blossoming of the arts, including theater.

The 1596 sketch of a play in progress at the Swan theater by Arnoldus Buchelius, based on a sketch by Johannes de Witt.

In addition to writing plays, Shakespeare acted in them. The role of the ghost in his play *Hamlet* is often considered to be his signature role. Do you think his career as an actor had any influence on his career as a playwright?

When Shakespeare died in 1616, he left his various relatives large sums of money or pieces of property, including his clothes, which he bequeathed to his sister. His wife, Anne, received the strangest item in his will—his "second-best bed." Scholars have spent many years wondering if this was an insult or a sign of deep and abiding love. We will probably never know.

The most important thing Shakespeare left behind was his work. His plays were first collected and published seven years after his death by his close friends, John Heminges and Henry Condell. These men were also involved in Shakespeare's acting company, Lord Chamberlain's Men. Their publication is called the First Folio, and without it, much of Shakespeare's work might have been lost forever.

READING SHAKESPEARE

Many people feel intimidated by Shakespeare. It can be hard to pick up one of his plays and just read it. Sometimes, it's difficult to understand what's happening, and some of his vocabulary and sentence structures feel alien to contemporary readers. It's different from what we're used to.

In addition to plays, Shakespeare wrote poetry, mostly sonnets. Sonnets are 14-line lyrical poems that usually follow a very specific rhythm called iambic pentameter. This rhythm has five pairs of syllables, an unstressed one followed by a stressed one.

> Shall I compare thee to a summer's day?
> Though art more lovely and more temperate:
> Rough winds do shake the darling buds of May,
> And summer's lease hath too short a date:
> Sometime too hot the eye of heaven shines,
> And often is his gold complexion dimm'd;
> And every fair from fair sometime declines,
> By chance or nature's changing course untrimm'd;
> But thy eternal summer shall not fade
> Nor lose possession of that fair thou ow'st;
> Nor shall Death brag thou wander'st in his shade,
> When in eternal lines to time thou growest:
> So long as men can breathe or eyes can see,
> So long lives this, and this gives life to thee.

In this poem, known as "Sonnet 18," the narrator is saying the subject of the poem is like the summer, only better. The subject is more lovely than a summer's day, and while summer is a short season, the subject's beauty will not fade, even after death, as long as there are people alive to read this poem.

FOLIO FACT

When you go to the movies, you buy your ticket at the box office. This term comes from Shakespeare's time, when the box of money from ticket sales was carried upstairs to an office to be counted.

THEATRE OR THEATER?

In England, the word *theater* is usually spelled theatre. *Colour* and *catalogue* are also examples of words with English spellings. When spelling first began to be standardized in the 1700s and 1800s, the two countries used different dictionaries and therefore have kept to different spellings.

While our theaters, audiences, costumes, music, and even the language are all different today from what they were 400 years ago, the very human reaction to tragedy, comedy, horror, and the strangeness of history are the same. By learning Shakespeare, we learn about ourselves.

The rhythm of "Sonnet 18," the same that's used in many of Shakespeare's plays, becomes more natural the more you read or listen to it. It's like hearing a song for the first time—as you become more familiar with the beat, the meaning of the lyrics become clearer and easier to understand.

That's why it can be useful to learn about Shakespeare through more modern work. It's pretty easy to figure out the plot of the movie *Warm Bodies*, and seeing that movie can help you figure out the meaning of the play *Romeo and Juliet*. Shakespeare wrote his plays for an audience—they were never meant to be read like novels. Hearing his lines spoken out loud, even in drastically different forms from the way he wrote them, such as with an undead theme, will make reading his lines easier and, perhaps, more inspiring.

[But why read Shakespeare at all? He lived so long ago, how can he still be relevant?]

Before Shakespeare, many plays were about characters named Morality, Charity, and Death. Can you figure out what those plays were about? Those plays aimed to teach audiences the difference between good and bad and to scare them into choosing good. The ones that have survived do not make for an inspiring theater experience and you don't see them performed very often on Broadway.

Instead, people flock to shows that feature complex characters and complicated plots. Viewers want plays that make them question themselves and the world around them. They want plays that make them feel emotions for characters that don't even exist, because the emotions themselves are very, very real.

Are you always good or always bad? Are you always right or always wrong? Probably not. Shakespeare understood that and wanted to show his audiences that they weren't alone in a sea of mixed emotions.

[
In this book, you'll explore the connections between contemporary work of today and four of Shakespeare's plays.
]

These plays include *Romeo and Juliet*, *Hamlet*, *Twelfth Night*, and *A Midsummer Night's Dream*. You'll learn to spot parallel themes, images, plot points, and characters. At the same time you'll gain a deeper understanding of his plays and how to read them.

We know so little about Shakespeare that it's hard to predict his likes and dislikes. From his work, we do know that he was an innovator who was excited about finding new ways of portraying the human experience. His characters also often struggle between the pull of tradition and the allure of revolution.

Would Shakespeare have liked the movie *Warm Bodies*? Would he have liked any of the contemporary retellings of his own plays? What do you think?

KEY QUESTIONS

- Why do we know so little about Shakespeare's life? Does it help or hurt to know about the author when you are studying his work?

- Have you ever seen a Shakespeare play performed? What did you think of it?

CREATE A SHAKESPEAREAN TIMELINE

Every writer, artist, musician, and other cultural visionary is at least partly a product of their time. What might the history of Shakespeare's era have contributed to the poems and plays he wrote that we enjoy today?

- **Use the timeline on this website to research milestones in Shakespeare's life.** Choose 10 major dates in Shakespeare's life and do some research into the events that happened around the world while Shakespeare was alive. Pay close attention to the events that happened during the years his plays were thought to have first been produced. You can try these websites for ideas.

🔍 absolute Shakespeare timeline

🔍 one day history

🔍 on this day history

- **Create a timeline showing those 10 major milestones and world events that happened at the same time.** Can you find events in both British history and American history to include? What about other parts of the world?

To investigate more, and as you become more familiar with the plays discussed in this book, refer back to your timeline and look for historic events that appear in his writing. Are there major historical figures that might have influenced his thoughts and ideas? Can you find similarities between any of Shakespeare's characters and the world leaders of the time? How does this change your reading of his plays?

Chapter One

Romeo and Juliet

Why is *Romeo and Juliet* still such a popular story?

Boy meets girl, boy and girl fall in love, boy and girl are kept apart— the plot of *Romeo and Juliet* is a timeless one that audiences of today still enjoy.

Do you think human nature has changed much in 400 years? Do people still behave the same way they did during Shakespeare's time? Scientists haven't invented a time machine yet, so the only evidence we have of human behavior from long ago is archaeological and artistic. We can study the artifacts that people left behind from different time periods, and we can look at paintings, music, sculpture, architecture, and literature to make educated guesses about what people did, how they did it, and why.

Shakespeare was a student of human nature. Through his plays, he presents studies of characters that show people behaving in many of the same ways in the Elizabethan Era as they do now.

Romeo and Juliet is a good example of this. A play about young, star-crossed lovers, the plot, characters, emotions, and themes are very familiar to contemporary audiences. This play has been adapted for stage, screen, and books more than a hundred times!

THE STORY

Romeo and Juliet is a story of two teenagers who fall in love. What makes their tale problematic and interesting is the bloody feud that's existed between their families for many generations. We learn this in the very first lines, or the prologue.

> Two households, both alike in dignity,
> In fair Verona, where we lay our scene,
> From ancient grudge break to new mutiny,
> Where civil blood makes civil hands unclean.
> From forth the fatal loins of these two foes
> A pair of star-cross'd lovers take their life;
> Whose misadventured piteous overthrows
> Do with their death bury their parents' strife.
> The fearful passage of their death-mark'd love,
> And the continuance of their parents' rage,
> Which, but their children's end,
> nought could remove,
> Is now the two hours' traffic of our stage;
> The which is you with patient ears attend,
> What here shall miss, our toil shall strive to mend.

The prologue gives away the entire plot of the play. The first four lines introduce the characters: "Two households"; the city in which they live: "fair Verona"; and the feud: "Ancient grudge break to new mutiny." We even learn that the main characters die in the end: "A pair of star-cross'd lovers take their life"; and how this affects their parents' feud: "Do with their death bury their parents' strife." We're also given a rough idea of how long the play will take: "two hours' traffic of our stage."

Something about *Romeo and Juliet* has resonated enough with people across the centuries that we keep revisiting it, enjoying it, and learning its lessons again and again.

FOLIO FACT

Hamlet is the longest of Shakespeare's plays with 4,024 lines. *Comedy of Errors* is the shortest with 1,786 lines. *Romeo and Juliet* is of average length with 3,093 lines.

CASA DI GIULIETTA

There is no evidence that Shakespeare ever traveled to Verona, and no evidence that a girl named Juliet lived in a house in Verona, but that hasn't stopped dreamers from around the world visiting one of Verona's major tourist attractions, the Casa di Giulietta. This thirteenth-century building, once an inn, belonged to the Capello family for many years before the city bought it and welcomed travelers to visit the site of a grand romance. A balcony that looks out over a courtyard is said to be the balcony where Juliet uttered her famous lines. A nearby brick wall hosts thousand of letters to Juliet, stuck there by lovelorn tourists looking for advice from one of the most famous lovers of all, Juliet.

The first scene of the first act of *Romeo and Juliet* opens with a fight in the streets of Verona between members of the Montague clan and members of the Capulet clan. Shakespeare sets a scene of violence before venturing into the subject of love. Why do you think he does this?

When Romeo first appears onstage, he is sad because the girl he loves, Rosaline, doesn't love him back. His friends scheme to bring Romeo to a party to cheer him up. Romeo agrees to go, but only because he knows Rosaline is going to be there and he wants to see her.

The party happens to be hosted by the Capulet family, the sworn enemies of the Montagues. By going to the party, Romeo and his friends risk being thrown out, or worse, attacked at sword point. This doesn't seem to bother them. Do you think it's human nature to value the chance of love above the chance of danger? Do you think people today still engage in risky behaviors for the sake of finding love or friendship?

When they get to the party, Romeo loses all memory of Rosaline when he spies Juliet across the room.

Did my heart love till now?
Forswear it, sight!
For I ne'er saw true beauty till this night.

(act 1 scene 5)

What do you think these lines mean? What is happening to him for the first time?

When Romeo and Juliet speak, Shakespeare displays their affection for each other by having them speak in the pattern of a sonnet. While people don't actually talk like that in real life, the passage works as a way to express how well they fit together.

Romeo: If I profane with my unworthiest hand
This holy shrine, the gentle sin is this:
My lips, two blushing pilgrims, ready stand
To smooth that rough touch with a tender kiss.

Juliet: Good pilgrim, you do wrong your hand
too much,
Which mannerly devotion shows in this;
For saints have hands that pilgrims' hands
do touch,
And palm to palm is holy palmers' kiss.

(act 1 scene 5)

When Juliet's cousin, Tybalt, realizes that Romeo is a Montague, he threatens to kill him. Romeo escapes, but later, Romeo sneaks into the Capulets' orchard and overhears Juliet, who is standing on her balcony, vowing to love Romeo forever even though he's a Montague.

Juliet: O Romeo, Romeo! wherefore art
thou Romeo?
Deny thy father and refuse thy name;
Or, if thou wilt not, be but sworn my love,
And I'll no longer be a Capulet.

Romeo: [Aside] Shall I hear more, or shall I
speak at this?

Juliet: 'Tis but thy name that is my enemy;
Thou art thyself, though not a Montague.
What's Montague? it is nor hand, nor foot,
Nor arm, nor face, nor any other part
Belonging to a man. O, be some other name!
What's in a name? that which we call a rose
By any other name would smell as sweet . . .

(act 2 scene 2)

photo credit: Spencer Wright

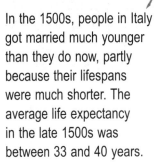

FOLIO FACT

In the 1500s, people in Italy got married much younger than they do now, partly because their lifespans were much shorter. The average life expectancy in the late 1500s was between 33 and 40 years.

Sadly, Romeo and Juliet are not a couple that's meant to be. They court for a day and then they get married. Quick? Yes, especially considering that Juliet is not quite 14 years old! While people got married and had families far earlier back then, that's still on the younger side of what was usual for the time.

[Shakespeare's audience already knew what was going to happen to the young lovers and were eager to see how it played out.]

Just as in so many great love stories, tragedy strikes. First, Romeo's best friend, Mercutio, is killed by the hand of Juliet's cousin, Tybalt, a Capulet.

This sparks a renewed flame in the war between Montagues and Capulets, which takes on greater stakes for the audience, since we know Romeo and Juliet have married and, in doing so, have grafted two branches of the different family trees together forever.

The families, however, don't know a thing about the marriage. Romeo, feeling that he failed to be brave enough when Mercutio was stabbed, fights and kills Tybalt. He is banished from Verona because of this. When Juliet can't stop weeping, her parents assume it's because of the death of her cousin, Tybalt. In reality, though, she's mourning the loss of her new husband, who has been exiled.

Juliet: Back, foolish tears, back to your native spring;
Your tributary drops belong to woe,
Which you, mistaking, offer up to joy.
My husband lives, that Tybalt would have slain;
And Tybalt's dead, that would have slain
my husband:
All this is comfort; wherefore weep I then?
Some word there was, worser than
Tybalt's death,
That murder'd me: I would forget it fain;
But, O, it presses to my memory,
Like damned guilty deeds to sinners' minds:
"Tybalt is dead, and Romeo—banished."
That "banished," that one word "banished,"
Hath slain ten thousand Tybalts.

(act 3 scene 2)

What is Juliet giving as the reason for her tears? What is she saying is worse than Tybalt's death?

Paris, one of Juliet's suitors who has been promised her hand in marriage, convinces Juliet's father to plan the wedding for that week. Juliet's grief is overwhelming, but her parents refuse to listen to her objections.

She turns to Friar Lawrence, who was the one who performed the secret wedding ceremony. Juliet obtains a concoction from him that will make her seem dead for a certain number of hours. Friar Lawrence promises that he'll write to Romeo and arrange for him to pick Juliet up at her tomb on the hour she's scheduled to wake from the sleeping draught.

Romeo's loss of his best friend, Mercutio, is a foreshadowing of his loss of Juliet.

The first page of *Romeo and Juliet* in the First Folio, 1623

JULIET'S NURSE

Another character that is important in the story is Juliet's nurse. Nurse provides some much-needed comic relief in the midst of tragedy. She has known Juliet since she was young and tells funny stories of Juliet as a child. Plus, she is the only character, other than Friar Lawrence, who knows about the relationship between Romeo and Juliet. Unfortunately, when Romeo is banished, Nurse urges Juliet to marry Paris, and Juliet decides to keep her plan of faking death a secret. If she'd trusted Nurse with the plan, the play could have been very different.

Juliet is buried on schedule, but the letter to Romeo never reaches him. He hears from another man that she's dead and rushes to her graveside, where he finds Paris mourning the dead Juliet. Paris mistakes Romeo for a vandal and attacks him, but in the battle, Romeo kills Paris. Instead of rescuing Juliet as he's supposed to, he kills himself with poison because he can't bear the thought of life without her. Juliet wakes, realizes that her beloved is dead, and stabs herself to death with one blow of Romeo's sword.

> **Juliet:** Yea, noise? then I'll be brief. O happy dagger!
> This is thy sheath; there rust, and let me die.
> *[She takes Romeo's dagger, stabs herself, and dies.]*
>
> (act 5 scene 3)

Can any good come out of this final scene? The families do decide to reconcile. They realize that the lives of their children were a high price to pay for an ongoing feud. Sadly, it's too late for Romeo and Juliet.

FATE VERSUS FREE WILL

The argument of fate versus free will has lasted as long as there have been humans to argue. In the prologue, Romeo and Juliet are described as "star-cross'd lovers." This means that their story, their fate, was written in the stars before they even met and fell in love. It also means they were doomed from the beginning to suffer a tragic tale.

What other works of literature address the topic of fate? Can you think of any movies or television shows in which fate plays a role in the story?

People in Shakespeare's time were great believers in fate. Many of them thought that no matter what you did, your actions and the results of those actions were predetermined. You were not in control of your own destiny—your destiny was already written in the stars.

Today, it's not as common for people to believe this. What do you think? Do you think Romeo and Juliet could have changed their fate and escaped their unhappy ending?

A TRAGICALL HISTORYE

Audiences in Shakespeare's time would probably have paid their pennies knowing how the final act turned out when they first went to see his play sometime between 1591 and 1595. This was already a familiar story to most people in the late 1500s, just as it's a familiar story to most people today.

As with most things having to do with Shakespeare, we don't really know for sure what inspired *Romeo and Juliet*. Most scholars agree, though, that Shakespeare was influenced by a 3,020-line poem titled "The Tragicall Historye of Romeus and Juliet" by Arthur Brooke, which was first published in 1562. Not much is known about Brooke, beyond the fact that he wrote the long poem about two young, star-crossed lovers and that he later died in a shipwreck.

There are many differences between the two pieces of literature. In Brooke's poem, the characters don't tend to appear until right before they're scheduled to do something dramatic and defining.

FOLIO FACT

The Oxford English Dictionary has credited Shakespeare with introducing almost 3,000 new words to the English language, including "frugal," "tranquil," and "bedroom."

For example, in Brooke's poem, Tybalt doesn't appear until his fight with Romeo, which ends in his death, while in Shakespeare's version, Tybalt appears early on as a rough-and-ready character aching for a fight.

[These changes make the action of the play more urgent and intense.]

The basic story of *Romeo and Juliet* stretches much farther into the past than Brooke's poem. There might even be some historical truth to the tale. Two families, the Montecchi and the Cappelletti, were political Italian families from the thirteenth century. They were mentioned in a famous poem called *The Divine Comedy*, written by an Italian writer named Dante.

A famous writer named Masuccio Salernitano published a story of young Italian lovers in a collection called *Il Novellino* in 1476, more than 100 years before Shakespeare's version. In 1530, Luigi da Porto published a book called *A Story Newly Found of Two Noble Lovers*, which names the characters as Romeo Montecchi and Giulietta Cappelletti.

FOLIO FACT

Brooke's poem takes place during a nine-month timeframe, while Shakespeare's plot unfolds between a Sunday and the following Thursday morning.

In 1554, Matteo Bandello published *Novelle*, which introduces the now-famous character of Juliet's nurse, who provides comic relief for the audience throughout the story.

We don't know if Shakespeare was familiar with all of these versions of the story of *Romeo and Juliet*. Scholars assume that he did know about Brooke's poem because it was published in England so soon before Shakespeare wrote his own play.

Today, writers and artists have to be careful about what they claim as their own writing. When you are assigned to write an essay for class, can you simply copy a piece of writing off the Internet or from a book? Instead, you read other essays and creative works to find information and inspiration to create your own work. That's exactly what people have been doing with Shakespeare's *Romeo and Juliet* since it was first performed, more than 400 years ago. In the next chapter, we'll look at some of those works and see how Shakespeare's language, characters, and themes are reflected in them.

COPYRIGHT!

Today, there are laws that protect writers from having their work plagiarized. These laws didn't exist in Shakespeare's time, and neither did the assumption that taking another writer's poem and changing it into your own play was a bad thing to do. Literature and art were freer to meander among the great minds of the time. On the other hand, more people know Shakespeare's name than they do Arthur Brooke's name. Do you think this is fair? Why or why not?

KEY QUESTIONS

- Why has the story of star-cross'd lovers endured for centuries?

- Who do you think was at fault for Romeo's and Juliet's deaths? Friar Lawrence? The nurse who knew about the marriage? Their parents? Only themselves?

- Why do you think their parents ended their feud right after discovering that their children were dead?

"A PLAGUE ON BOTH YOUR HOUSES"

In Shakespeare's time, sometimes the cure for disease was as bad as the disease itself. Elizabethan doctors believed that our bodies contained four different humors, or fluids—blood, phlegm, choler (or yellow bile), and melancholy (or black bile). Doctors thought that disease was caused by these humors becoming unbalanced. To bring the fluids back to a balanced state, doctors would try to release or add more of a fluid from the body. Often, patients died of whatever cure the doctor prescribed.

VOCAB LAB

Write down what you think each word means: **theme, resonate, feud, prologue, sonnet, foreshadowing, comic relief, reconcile,** and **predetermined**.

Compare your definitions with those of your friends or classmates. Did you all come up with the same meanings? Turn to the text and glossary if you need help.

Check your answers in the resources in the back of this book.

• **Try and guess which of the following practices were actual Elizabethan cures for disease.**

a. Applying leeches to the skin to suck out blood

b. Cutting open the buboes and pressing a poultice of butter, onion, and garlic to the skin

c. Inhaling steam made from boiling water and cow manure

d. Treating the infected area with boiled oil

e. Cleaning the cut with vinegar

f. Inserting roasted onions in the patient's ear

g. Transfusing the patient with the blood of a lamb

h. Grinding acorns and sprinkling the powder over a cut

i. Smearing a hot bandage with honey and pigeon dung

j. Drinking pig urine

k. Making a pilgrimage to a holy site

l. Drinking liquor

m. Drinking a tea made of lavender and rosemary

n. Applying a mixture of mud and ear wax

o. Soaking in a tub of human blood

p. Sleeping a night out in the cold

q. Drinking wine mixed with crow feces

r. Eating the chopped meat of geese and kittens

Chapter Two ▶

The Romeos and Juliets of Today

WH–WHEREFORE ART THINE BRAINS?

What are some of the ways artists and writers have reinterpreted *Romeo and Juliet*?

Romeo and Juliet is an enduring love story that has inspired more than 100 different versions of the story in books, movies, and music.

Many movies, books, and even songs have their roots in the enduring play of *Romeo and Juliet*. Why? Part of the reason is that it's such a good story. People enjoy tales about people falling in love and encountering different roadblocks, such as warring families or a zombie apocalypse.

While it's entertaining to watch the movies and read the books that have their roots in Shakespeare's work, it's also a good way to learn more about the plays they're based on. By finding the common elements and discovering what is different and why the artists made those choices, we can better understand the original plays and the lasting effect they've had on our culture.

WARM BODIES

The 2013 movie *Warm Bodies* follows the story of R, who is a zombie. He doesn't remember who he was or what his life was like before he became a zombie.

He lives in a world where many people are zombies, and those who aren't live behind a very high wall designed to keep the zombies out.

Julie is from behind that wall. She's not a zombie. In fact, her father is a leader in the walled community, the one who dictates when it's safe for raiding parties to leave the enclosure to get food, medicine, and other supplies. Julie and her boyfriend, Perry, are on one of these raiding parties when R and his fellow zombies attack Julie's group and R eats Perry's brains, as zombies do. When R spots Julie, it's love at first sight, just like in *Romeo and Juliet*.

R takes Julie back to his home. He lives in an airplane at an airport, which is where the zombies tend to hang out. He feeds her, plays music for her, drives a car with her, and cares for her. He finally realizes that he needs to let her go so that she'll be safe.

By then, Julie has realized that R is different from the other zombies and she is reluctant to leave. But if she doesn't leave, she faces certain death at the hands of zombies. She returns home to her family and friends, where she tries to convince her father that there's hope for the zombies and, therefore, all of humanity. R follows and tries to help her, even while hiding his true identity under makeup.

[
"Don't be creepy. Don't be creepy. Don't be creepy," R thinks to himself as he tries to pass for normal in front of an armed guard.
]

While Shakespeare's characters Romeo and Juliet confronted significant obstacles in the form of the rift between their families, R and Julie face what seem like insurmountable odds—a dystopian future in which their respective colonies are battling each other for limited resources.

The movie doesn't travel all the way down the path of tragedy. Instead of being banished as Romeo was, R runs away with Julie and amasses an army of zombies, all of whom are feeling more human since one of their own fell in love. Instead of committing a double suicide, R and Julie dive into a pool to escape certain death. They manage to survive, even thrive, as the humans finally understand that R isn't the danger they thought he was. *Warm Bodies* is the kind of romance that ends on a feel-good note—the wall comes down, the zombies are welcomed into society and learn to eat vegetables, and R and Julie live happily ever after.

Despite this swerve in the ending, there are many similarities between *Warm Bodies* and *Romeo and Juliet*. The character of the nurse, who provides plenty of comedy in Shakespeare's play, appears in *Warm Bodies* as Julie's friend, Nora.

Nora has many of the funnier lines of the play. When she learns that Julie is attracted to R, she says, "I mean, I know it's really hard to meet guys right now, with the apocalypse and stuff. Trust me. And, like, I know that you miss Perry. But, Julie, this is just weird. Like, I wish the Internet was still working so I could just look up whatever it is that's wrong with you."

Just as Romeo has a funny, fiery friend named Mercutio, R has a friend named M. He introduces M with the lines, "This is my best friend. By best friend, I mean we occasionally grunt and stare awkwardly at each other. We even have almost conversations sometimes." M becomes R's closest ally as they struggle to be valued in the human world. Mercutio dies in the play, while zombie M lives on to enjoy the transition into something more human.

Perhaps the clearest connection between *Warm Bodies* and *Romeo and Juliet* is the ending. While the stories end very differently, there is a resolution in *Warm Bodies* that echoes the final realization among the parents of the star-crossed lovers. Julie and R watch as the wall between the human world and the zombie world is blown to bits, signifying the integration of the two societies. In Romeo and Juliet, the parents who are left after so many characters have died resolve to end the dispute between the families, which has been like a wall between them.

GNOMEO & JULIET

One of the most accessible movie renditions of *Romeo and Juliet* is *Gnomeo & Juliet*. This feature-length animation explores the division between the red garden gnomes and the blue garden gnomes, who express their discontent with each other through lawnmower races.

When Juliet, from the red garden, meets Gnomeo, from the blue garden, they don't quite fall in love at first sight, but it's close. With the help of Featherstone, a one-legged plastic flamingo, they continue to meet outside the boundaries of the gardens, where they don't have to worry about their love being discovered by their friends or families.

Remember the balcony scene in Shakespeare's *Romeo and Juliet*, in which Juliet laments the fact that the one she loves is a Montague? There's a version of her speech in *Gnomeo & Juliet* as well.

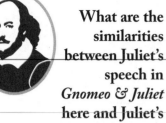

What are the similarities between Juliet's speech in *Gnomeo & Juliet* here and Juliet's speech in *Romeo and Juliet* on page 17?

Oh, Gnomeo, Gnomeo, are we really doomed to never see each other again? Why must you wear a blue hat? Why couldn't it be red like my father, or green like . . . like a leprechaun . . . or purple like, ummm, like some weird guy—I mean what's in a gnome? Because you are blue, my father sees red, and because I am red, I am feeling blue. Oh, at any rate that shouldn't be the thing to keep us apart, should it?

Unfortunately, the two love-struck gnomes are discovered. It happens at just about the same time a particularly feisty garden gnome manages to order a monster lawn mower off the Internet and wreak havoc to both gardens. Juliet, glued to the top of a fountain, is in immediate danger, but Gnomeo rushes to the rescue. When the dust settles, both families are heartbroken to see a pile of rubble where their beloved children once stood.

Because this is a movie for kids, Gnomeo & Juliet burst out of the top of the mess, alive and well. There is much rejoicing and Gnomeo & Juliet get married and ride off into the sunset on a purple lawnmower. Because, what do you get when you mix red and blue?

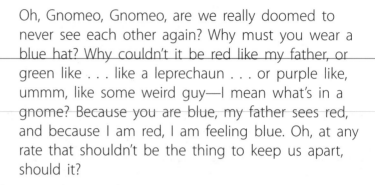

Shakespeare himself makes an appearance in *Gnomeo & Juliet*. He's a statue that comes to life to give advice to the doomed couple. He observes that Gnomeo's story is similar to another.

Shakespeare's statue: Your story, it does put me in mind of another.

Gnomeo: It does?

Shakespeare's statue: Oh! Indeed! Yes, there are remarkable similarities.

Gnomeo: What happens? Do they get back together then?

Shakespeare's statue: Get back together? Um . . . No, not exactly.

Gnomeo: What exactly do you mean?

Shakespeare's statue: Well, now, it really is quite good. She feigns her death. He finds her, thinks her dead, takes his own life. She wakes, find him dead, takes her life, both dead! Exeunt omnes, the end, curtain! Standing ovation! Bravo! Bravo! Author! Author!

Gnomeo: What did you say? They both die? What kind of an ending is that?

Shakespeare's statue: My dear boy, it is a tragedy.

This type of scene uses a literary device called metafiction. Books and movies that contain metafiction are stories that reference themselves within the text. *Gnomeo & Juliet* is a movie based on a play by Shakespeare, so when a Shakespeare character talks about a play he wrote, the plot of which is being performed by the gnomes that surround him, it's metafiction.

[
Metafiction provides a way for the audience to reflect on what they're watching.
]

MORE METAFICTION

There are many children's books that use metafiction. For example, in the book, *We Are In a Book* by Mo Williams, the characters Piggy and Gerald suspect that they are in a book and being watched by a reader. They worry about what will happen when the book ends. *Harold and the Purple Crayon* is another example of a picture book that uses metafiction. Harold, the main character, uses his purple crayon to draw the scenes of the book he's in. Lemony Snicket also used metafiction in his books. In *A Series of Unfortunate Events*, he continually warns the reader that, "In this book, not only is there no happy ending, there is no happy beginning and very few happy things in the middle."

There are many other examples of *Romeo and Juliet* being transformed into movies. The movie and play *West Side Story* places the plot of *Romeo and Juliet* into New York City in the 1950s. *West Side Story* frames the plot around the rivalry between two gangs, the Jets and the Sharks. Why do you think Shakespeare's play works well as a film? What parts of the play do you think producers find interesting?

BOOKS

Shakespeare's most famous love story didn't inspire just movies. There is a useful dichotomy to the plot, which means there are two sides joined by a link—the couple that falls in love. This makes it a good play to use for stories about different groups at war with each other, with many different groups representing the two families.

In the book, *Street Love*, by Walter Dean Myers, Junice and Damien come from very different Harlem families. Damien is a good student from a two-parent family who has been accepted to Brown University.

A fight scene from a 1957 Broadway performance of *West Side Story*

photo credit: Fred Fehl

Junice, on the other hand, is just trying to keep her younger sister and grandmother living together as a family after their mother is sent to jail.

Despite the wide socioeconomic gap between them, Damien and Junice fall in love. However, the reality of their divergent futures is a lot of pressure for a teenage couple. The differences between one successful and well-off family and the other struggling family are simply too great.

> Just as Romeo and Juliet were undermined by the relationship between their families, Damien and Junice are stymied by the gulf between the families they were born into.

Street Love is written in short, free-verse poems that sometimes reflect hip-hop beats and rhythms. Damien and Junice would have heard these from boom boxes on the street corners and basketball courts of urban Harlem. The poetry can also be construed as a nod toward Shakespeare, who wove poetry into his plays.

"LOVE STORY"

Taylor Swift's song "Love Story" captures Juliet's desperation to be with her beloved Romeo with key lyrics that reflect the plot of Shakespeare's play.

"Little did I know...

That you were Romeo, you were throwing pebbles, And my daddy said, 'Stay away from Juliet,' And I was crying on the staircase Begging you, 'Please don't go,' And I said...

Romeo, take me somewhere we can be alone. I'll be waiting; all that's left to do is run. You'll be the prince and I'll be the princess, It's a love story, baby, just say, 'Yes.'"

🔍 Taylor Swift Love Story

This section of poem is in the voice of Damien.

I have never felt so alone
Cogito ergo sum; I think, therefore I am
Dead thoughts in a dead language
What good is thinking? What good is *I am*
If *I am* is not something larger
Than I could ever be alone?
The thinking, the furrowed brow
Had always been, until this time
A comfort.
To this very moment every
Red horizon produced a new day
Every cloud its cleansing shower
The sun never stopped its
Brilliant arcing across my blue skies
What strange land have I entered

Meyers captures the plot of *Romeo and Juliet* in his short, free-verse novel. He also manages to combine some of the rhythm of the original play into a form young audiences today might find similar to rap music.

Another book that follows the plot and characterizations of *Romeo and Juliet* is *Romiette and Julio* by Sharon M. Draper. Romiette is an African American living in Cincinnati, and Julio is an Hispanic teen whose family moves from Texas to Cincinnati to get away from the gang violence. Unfortunately, Cincinnati has its share of gangs as well, and Julio soon find himself at the center of a controversy that stems, in part, because of his interracial relationship with Romiette.

Romiette and Julio plays with language in a way that Shakespeare might have appreciated. Several of the chapters are told in online, chatroom dialogue, which is how the two main characters meet.

niobe: We just read Hamlet in school. EVERYBODY dies.

becool: who cares?

oogaooga: Shakespeare is stupid.

afroqueen: it's not so bad.

spanishlover: you into Shakespeare?

cookieman: Shakespeare was a dude!

niobe: so was Charles Manson—what's your point?

vanityfair: suppose Shakespeare was a woman?

Sweetthing: maybe he was.

becool: who cares!

bigmac: would we still have to read that stuff in school?

afroqueen: no—cause nobody paid any attention to women back then!

cookieman: nobody pays any attention now.

Reinterpretation of a play is a way for contemporary writers, movie makers, and singers to creatively explore old material and find ways of making it feel new and vital to modern audiences. While people still attend the traditional play *Romeo and Juliet* in droves, it's also important to see the play as a vehicle for other types of creative engagement. Even Shakespeare did this when he used "The Tragicall Historye of Romeus and Juliet" to present a timeless story in a new and different way.

By watching, reading, and listening to retellings of *Romeo and Juliet*, we can apply the lessons of the play to the kinds of situations that didn't even exist in Shakespeare's time. This includes teenagers struggling to survive the dangerous neighborhood of Harlem or garden gnomes trying to find love.

VOCAB LAB

Write down what you think each word means: **discern, insurmountable, dystopian, animosity, laments, metafiction, dichotomy, divergent,** and **stymied.**

Compare your definitions with those of your friends or classmates. Did you all come up with the same meanings? Turn to the text and glossary if you need help.

KEY QUESTIONS

- Why do you think *Romeo and Juliet* has so many different interpretations?

- How does the role of the nurse change in different versions of the play? Can you think of other books and movies that portray this type of role?

DROP THE BEAT

Rap music is spoken word poetry set to music. Many rap songs make use of couplets, or two lines together that rhyme. If Shakespeare was alive today, he'd probably like rap music, because it's a creative way to express ideas to lots of different people, which is what he tried to do with his plays. In this activity, try to find your own muse and set the story of *Romeo and Juliet* in a rap song.

- **Find an app that provides looping beats to download on your phone or other device.** You can also make a beat using your hands to clap or by tapping a pencil on the table.

- **Reflect back on the story of *Romeo and Juliet*.** Is there a part of their story that you found more interesting than others? What do you think it would have been like to be in their characters? Have you ever had any experiences like theirs?

- **Start talking about your favorite part of *Romeo and Juliet* with one short sentence.** Add another line to your first sentence and make them rhyme. Use the beat to find a rhythm that feels right to you.

- **If it's difficult to speak your lines, write them down first and then speak them out loud.** Feel free to change them when you're speaking them. Rap music tends to be fluid and dynamic. It adapts to the moment.

- **Write a song that's as long as you want it to be.** Play with different rhythms to find a couple that you can use in one song to make it interesting. Use your device to record your rap song and share it with others.

To investigate more, write a rap song about your own experiences. You don't have to write about love—you can write about anything that sparks emotion for you. Some ideas include friendship, difficulty with family members, your feelings about disasters or political upheaval in other countries, and your hopes for your own future.

Chapter Three ▶

The Tragedy of Hamlet, Prince of Denmark

What makes *Hamlet* an enduring tragedy?

The character in *Hamlet* shows many emotions that audiences might recognize in themselves, including grief, anger, love, and the desire for revenge.

Hamlet is widely considered to be Shakespeare's greatest tragedy, perhaps his greatest play. He wrote it sometime between 1599 and 1601, and some scholars say it's his most personal work. Remember, his son was named Hamnet, a name that was used interchangeably with Hamlet back in Shakespeare's time. His son died in 1596 when he was 11 years old. Scholars say that it was this loss that made Shakespeare able to write about the extreme depths of despair in the tragedies he produced in the years after his son's death.

In *Hamlet*, most of the characters die by the end of the play, but that isn't what makes this Shakespeare's most accomplished tragedy. It is Hamlet's emotional state and his inability to make a decision and act upon that decision that make this a sad play to read or see on stage.

THE STORY

In the play, Hamlet's father, the king of Denmark, has died a month before the action begins. While Hamlet is grieving for his father, his main emotion is anger at his mother's marriage to his uncle, Claudius, very soon after his father's death. He even suspects that Claudius had a hand in his father's death. Was the quick marriage planned from the beginning? He is angry with both his uncle and his mother, on top of being devastated about the loss of his father.

Hamlet begins with the appearance of a spirit. In the play, the ghost appears to the men keeping watch over Elsinore castle, where the royal Danish family resides.

The ghost remains silent until several scenes later, when Hamlet finds out that it's been appearing to the night watch and decides to investigate for himself. The ghost reveals to Hamlet that he is Hamlet's dead father and goes on to describe how he died.

> Brief let me be. Sleeping within my orchard,
> My custom always of the afternoon,
> Upon my secure hour thy uncle stole,
> With juice of cursed hebenon in a vial,
> And in the porches of my ears did pour
> The leperous distilment; whose effect
> Holds such an enmity with blood of man
> That swift as quicksilver it courses through
> The natural gates and alleys of the body,
> And with a sudden vigour doth posset
> And curd, like eager droppings into milk,
> The thin and wholesome blood: so did it mine.

(act 1 scene 5)

ENTER SHAKESPEARE

The ghost is the role most often associated with Shakespeare. Remember, Shakespeare was an actor as well as a playwright, and scholars believe he often played the role of the ghost.

FOLIO FACT

"Thus was I, sleeping, by a brother's hand / Of life, of crown, of queen, at once dispatch'd." Here, the ghost says his brother killed him, removed his crown, and took his wife, the queen, from him all at the same time.

What is the ghost describing? What happened to Hamlet's father while he napped in the orchard?

[**The ghost asks Hamlet to avenge his murder, and Hamlet agrees.**]

However, Hamlet is conflicted about whether or not the ghost is telling the truth about being poisoned. He decides to keep his suspicions about the true nature of his father's death secret and to watch his uncle carefully. He needs proof that his uncle did indeed plot to murder the king, marry the queen, and secure the crown for himself. In the meantime, Hamlet acts insane so that he appears harmless.

His plot seems to work. His friends and family begin to think he's lost his mind. Hamlet's girlfriend, Ophelia, tells her father, Polonius, one of the king's advisors, that Hamlet visited her in her chambers and acted very strangely:

And with a look so piteous in purport
As if he had been loosed out of hell
To speak of horrors—he comes before me.

(act 2 scene 1)

Polonius takes this as proof of Hamlet's insanity, and tells Gertrude and Claudius. The two of them engage the help of two of Hamlet's old friends, Rosencrantz and Guildenstern, to spy on Hamlet and determine if he has gone crazy. Hamlet, however, sees through their plot. He says to them:

You were sent for; and there is a kind of confession in your looks
which your modesties have not craft enough to colour:
I know the good king and queen have sent for you.

(act 2 scene 2)

DOWN THE HATCH

New medical discoveries are being made every day, just as they were in Shakespeare's time. One major discovery in the 1500s was made by a doctor named Bartolomeo Eustachio, which he described in his book *De Auditus Organis*. He discovered the Eustachian tube, named after himself, that runs between the ear canal and the throat. This could be the inspiration behind Shakespeare's idea of having Claudius murder King Hamlet with the odd technique of pouring poison in his ear.

Hamlet doesn't trust his old friends, but he knows he must act as though he's happy they're visiting. Luckily, a group of players arrives at the castle to perform and this provides a distraction. Hamlet convinces the actors to put on a play with a plot that directly reflects what he thinks happened to his father. If Claudius shows guilt while watching the play, that will prove he murdered the King of Denmark.

["The play's the thing / Wherein I'll catch the conscience of the King," says Hamlet.]

Hamlet's plan works, perhaps too well. Claudius is very uncomfortable during the play, called *The Mousetrap*. The queen is uncomfortable as well, which makes Hamlet wonder how involved his mother was in his father's death. He meets with his mother in her room, while, unknown to Hamlet, Polonius hides behind the curtain to spy. Hamlet acts crazy and accusatory in his mother's room.

Queen Gertrude: Hamlet, thou hast thy father much offended.

Hamlet: Mother, you have my father much offended.

Queen Gertrude: Come, come, you answer with an idle tongue.

Hamlet: Go, go, you question with a wicked tongue.

Queen Gertrude: Why, how now, Hamlet!

Hamlet: What's the matter now?

Queen Gertrude: Have you forgot me?

Hamlet: No, by the rood, not so:
You are the queen, your husband's brother's wife;
And—would it were not so!—you are my mother.

(act 3 scene 4)

Many people believe that other people are more likely to tell the truth in front of a person they don't think capable of understanding anything. Do you agree?

FOLIO FACT

Hamlet is Shakespeare's longest play, with more than 4,000 lines to it. On stage, an uncut or unedited production can run for four hours, although many productions are under two hours.

Queen Gertrude is horrified by her son's crazy behavior and frightened for her own life. She calls for help and Polonius, still behind the curtain, answers. Hamlet mistakes Polonius for King Claudius and draws his rapier to thrust it through the curtain at the figure, accidentally striking Polonius dead.

Because of Polonius's death, Ophelia, his daughter, goes crazy, and she isn't faking it as Hamlet is doing. During a meeting with the queen, she can do nothing but sing silly songs and utter lines that make no sense. Later, she drowns herself, burdened by her father's death and perhaps feeling abandoned by Hamlet.

Ophelia's brother, Laertes, already furious with Hamlet for killing their father, vows revenge for his sister's death as well. He has to wait, though, since Claudius has sent Hamlet to England with a letter ordering Hamlet's own death. Hamlet believes he is being sent away as a punishment for killing Polonius. His friends-turned-spies, Rosencrantz and Guildenstern, accompany him.

On the way, they observe Fortinbras, son of the elder Fortinbras, the king of Norway, who was killed by Hamlet's father. The younger Fortinbras is on his way to Denmark to avenge his own father's death.

One of the most famous depictions of Ophelia, painted by John Everett Millais, 1851

photo credit: Tate, London, 2011

Hamlet notices a difference in Fortinbras's approach to revenge and his own approach. While Hamlet can't bring himself to actually act on his promise of revenge, Fortinbras is going about it with focus and determination, amassing an army to invade the offending country. Hamlet considers the differences between them in this soliloquy.

> Why yet I live to say 'This thing's to do;'
> Sith I have cause and will and strength and means
> To do't. Examples gross as earth exhort me;
> Witness this army of such mass and charge
> Led by a delicate and tender prince,
> Whose spirit divine ambition puff'd
> Makes mouths at the invisible event….

(act 4 scene 4)

[**What does Hamlet see as the difference between himself and Fortinbras?**]

When pirates overtake the traveling threesome, Hamlet uses the opportunity to plant a letter on his companions with instructions to the king to have them killed, and escapes. He heads back to Denmark, meeting the loyal Horatio on the way.

Close to Elsinore, they come across grave diggers preparing a site for Ophelia. Hamlet picks up the skull of Yorick, who served as jester during his father's reign.

> Alas, poor Yorick! I knew him, Horatio: a fellow of infinite jest, of most excellent fancy: he hath borne me on his back a thousand times; and now, how abhorred in my imagination it is! my gorge rims at it. Here hung those lips that I have kissed I know not how oft.

(act 5 scene 1)

[
Hamlet doesn't have long to wonder about his own mortality.
]

Claudius and Laertes have plotted Hamlet's death. Laertes challenges Hamlet to a sword fight, but what Hamlet doesn't know is that Laertes is using a sword that's been dipped in poison. Even if Hamlet gets only a scratch, he'll die from it.

Just in case, Claudius has also filled a goblet with poison to feed to Hamlet if he's still living after the fight. Unfortunately for Gertrude, this is the glass she drinks from to praise her son's good fighting. And then the swords get switched in the confusion of the dual and Hamlet rams Laertes's own sword into him, causing Laertes to die, too.

With his last breath, Laertes admits to Hamlet that Claudius was the one who killed Hamlet's father. Finally, Hamlet finds the clarity and strength to exact the revenge he promised many scenes ago. He kills Claudius, and then Hamlet dies as well from a scratch from Laertes's poisoned sword.

Only Horatio, Hamlet's good friend, escapes death in the final scene of the play. Why do you think Shakespeare killed off most of the characters in the play? How do you think Horatio felt being the last person left alive?

THEMES IN HAMLET

One of the most famous lines in *Hamlet* is spoken by Polonius, the advisor to the king and the father of Hamlet's girlfriend, Ophelia. He is giving advice to his son, Laertes, who is about to leave for school.

> This above all: to thine own self be true,
> And it must follow, as the night the day,
> Thou canst not then be false to any man.
>
> (act 1 scene 3)

"To thine own self be true"—what do you think this means? In today's world, people say this to mean, "Be true to yourself." Do what you feel is right, even if other people try to get you to behave differently. In Shakespeare's time, the phrase meant something very different.

When Polonius says, "To thine own self be true," he is telling his son to only act in ways that improve his own life, to be selfish. Take care of yourself first, he is saying, and then you'll be able to take care of others.

For the characters in Hamlet, this advice comes up over and over. Hamlet struggles with the question of how to be the best son. Is killing Claudius to avenge his father's death the right thing to do? Does failing to do this make him a bad son?

> And as Hamlet acts insane to fool people into telling him the truth, does the act overtake him and make him truly mad?

What if Hamlet were to follow Polonius's advice to take care of himself above all others? Hamlet might not have had such a hard time pursuing the vengeance he promised the ghost of his father.

POOR YORICK

Hamlet's speech to Yorick's skull is one of the most famous in literary history. You can see a clip of this scene from the 1990 movie of *Hamlet* here.

🔍 Mel Gibson Poor Yorick

HAMLET IN KLINGON

Hamlet has been translated into more than 80 languages, including Klingon, the language of an alien race in the popular science fiction movie franchise *Star Trek*. You can listen to some of the Klingon version of the play and hear actors discussing how they performed the play in Klingon at this website.

🔍 Klingons Shakespeare video

Hamlet's nature is not a vengeful one. We know this from comparing his character to that of both Laertes and Fortinbras, who find themselves in similar situations. When Hamlet kills Polonius, Laertes doesn't hesitate to vow to kill Hamlet, and sets about arranging a quick death. Fortinbras, too, shows a focused desire to avenge his father's death, and even rallies an army to help ensure it happens.

Hamlet, on the other hand, spends five acts wondering if killing Claudius is the right thing to do. Do you think the reason Hamlet hesitates is because he's taking care of himself or because he's trying to take care of his father's memory?

Mortality is another theme that Shakespeare explores in *Hamlet*. Many people die in this play, but more importantly, many people think about what happens after death. Remember, Shakespeare wrote this a few years after his son's death. Do you think he would have been thinking about the meaning of death during this time?

Early in the play, Hamlet remarks on the nature of death in his famous soliloquy.

> To be, or not to be: that is the question:
> Whether 'tis nobler in the mind to suffer
> The slings and arrows of outrageous fortune,
> Or to take arms against a sea of troubles,
> And by opposing end them? To die: to sleep;
> No more; and by a sleep to say we end
> The heart-ache and the thousand natural shocks
> That flesh is heir to, 'tis a consummation
> Devoutly to be wish'd. To die, to sleep;
> To sleep: perchance to dream: ay, there's the rub;
> For in that sleep of death what dreams may come
> When we have shuffled off this mortal coil,
> Must give us pause: there's the respect
> That makes calamity of so long life....

(act 3 scene 1)

Hamlet is so upset by his father's death, his mother's marriage to his uncle, and his own role of avenger that he's considering killing himself. He's questioning which is better, life or death? Is it better to sleep forever, and ". . . by a sleep to say we end the heart-ache and the thousand natural shocks that flesh is heir to . . ."? Hamlet is saying that death brings an end to feeling bad, and that might be preferable to living.

However, he also acknowledges that no one knows what comes after death. It might be worse: "For in that sleep of death what dreams may come when we have shuffled off this mortal coil, must give us pause . . . ." Hamlet comes to the conclusion that even when life is hard and hurtful, it's better to deal with what you know than suffer what could be worse.

RICHARD BURBAGE

Richard Burbage (1567-1619) was the first actor to perform Hamlet's famous soliloquy that begins, "To be or not to be." He is one of the most famous actors to perform at the Globe Theatre, of which he was part owner. He continued to act with the King's Men acting company until his death in 1619, when the outpouring of public grief almost reached the level of grief people had showed Queen Anne only 10 days before. His gravestone is said to have read, "Exit Burbage."

HOW HAMLET CAME TO BE

Just as the people who went to see *Romeo and Juliet* in 1595 were familiar with the plot of the play, the audience of *Hamlet* in 1601 might have known the story they'd be viewing.

A similar story can be found as early as 1200 in a Scandinavian tale called *Vita Amlethi*, named by a modern translator but written by a writer named Saxo Grammaticus. *Vita Amlethi* is about a boy named Amleth, whose father, the king, is killed and whose mother remarries the dead king's brother soon after. Amleth is a young boy at the time of the murder, but he senses that he is in grave danger if it becomes known that he suspects his uncle of murder.

To fool his family, he pretends to be mad, and spends his days sitting on the floor whittling tiny arrows.

> Unlike Hamlet, who can't bring himself to kill his uncle, Amleth bides his time until he's able to use the thousands of tiny daggers he's carved over the years to take his revenge.

There are many similarities between the two tales, such as a young girl being used as a test of madness, the killing of a hidden spy, and the sending of two men to be killed in Amleth's place.

Just as Shakespeare used material from earlier works, there are movies and books we enjoy today that use the plot of Hamlet in different ways. We'll take a look at some of these in the next chapter.

KEY QUESTIONS

- Why did Hamlet hesitate to kill his uncle and get revenge for his father's death?

- Do you think Hamlet's mother, Gertrude, was an active part of the plot? Do you think she had anything to do with King Hamlet's death?

TO WRITE OR NOT TO WRITE

Hamlet contains what might be the most famous speech in English literature—"To be or not to be; that is the question." We looked at what Hamlet was thinking about when he made the speech at the graveyard, but what does the whole speech mean?

- **Read through the speech several times and figure out what Hamlet is saying.** The best way to understand Shakespeare's writing is to take it line by line and pay attention to where the sentences begin and end. Shakespeare used metaphors and similes to describe things, so the nouns in his writing might represent other things. He often mixed parts of sentences around so that it would be spoken in a different way from what people usually said.

- **Rewrite Hamlet's speech with wording that people today can immediately understand.** Try to interpret each line. Look up words you don't know in the dictionary.

- **Speak your version out loud, and then speak Shakespeare's original out loud.** How do they sound different? Which do you like better? Which do you think audiences would like better?

> To investigate more, try this exercise with other speeches in the play. Does it get easier the more you do it? Are you better able to understand the concept of what Shakespeare is saying even when you don't know the meanings of every word or understand all the references?

Inquire & Investigate

VOCAB LAB

Write down what you think each word means: **soliloquy**, **Eustachian tube**, **rapier**, **burden**, **amass**, **inevitable**, **clarity**, and **ritual**.

Compare your definitions with those of your friends or classmates. Did you all come up with the same meanings? Turn to the text and glossary if you need help.

You can find Hamlet's entire "To be or not to be" speech at this website.

🔍 Shakespeare MIT Hamlet to be or not to be

Chapter Four ▶

The Hamlets of Today

TO HAKUNA OR NOT TO HAKUNA, THAT IS THE QUESTION...

How has the story of *Hamlet* influenced recent works of art?

Artwork, many books, and films, including a Disney production, have been inspired by some of the plot elements of *Hamlet*.

"Awimbawe, awimbawe, awimbawe . . . ." In 1994, Disney released the movie *The Lion King*, inspiring a generation of young people to try their skill at singing the high-pitched notes of the song, "In the Jungle." Some of these young people might have been inspired to read *Hamlet*, too. Why? Because *The Lion King* is based on *Hamlet*!

Many movies, books, and television series are based on *Hamlet*, for several different reasons. First, the plot of revenge is a timeless one. As individuals we try to be the best people we can be and keep ourselves from reacting to situations in ways that can only mean harm. But revenge is a very popular theme in all kinds of art.

Another reason *Hamlet* is so popular is the characters. Who doesn't know what it's like to be caught in a trap of paralyzing indecision? Audiences can identify with the character of Hamlet, because within most people there lies a sense of uncertainty.

THE LION KING

The Lion King is a full-length animated movie featuring lions, hyenas, a meerkat, and a warthog. Simba the lion is only a child when his father, Mufasa, is killed by stampeding wildebeests. Simba believes himself to be responsible for Mufasa's death and runs away, though it was really Simba's uncle, Scar, who caused the stampede and threw Mufasa into the path of the dangerous animals. Luckily for Simba, two adventurous African creatures, Timon and Pumbaa, find him and save him from certain death in the desert.

Some time later, after Simba has grown a mane and deepened his voice, he meets another lion and recognizes his childhood sweetheart, Nala. She tells him what life has been like since his father died and Scar became king. Food and water are scarce, hyenas run rampant over the pride lands, and the herd is dying.

> Nala wants Simba to return to Pride Rock and challenge Scar, taking his rightful place as king of the lions.

Simba, however, isn't interested, Simba has adopted the motto of his two friends, Timon and Pumbaa—*hakuna matata*. It means you don't have to worry about anything, that you can spend your days playing, eating, and enjoying yourself without thinking about the problems of the rest of the world. Does this sound like a useful way to live your life?

THE LION KING

The MPAA has rated this movie G for all audiences.

FOLIO FACT

The Lion King was originally titled, *The King of the Jungle*. But where do lions live? Not in the jungle!

FOLIO FACT

It is a sign of *Hamlet's* strength as a play that it can be adapted into a widely different piece of art.

Nala isn't impressed at Simba's refusal to take responsibility, and she and Simba fight over it. Simba runs off and meets a wise monkey, Rafiki, who plays a character similar to the fool. The fool doesn't appear in *Hamlet*, except as a skull. In many of Shakespeare's other plays, though, the fool acted as both a comedic interruption to heavy drama and as the voice of clarity.

Rafiki: The question is, who . . . are you?

Adult Simba: I thought I knew, but now I'm not so sure.

Rafiki: Well, I know who you are! Shh. Come here, it's a secret. *Asante sana Squash banana, Wiwi nugu Mi mi apana!*

Adult Simba: Enough already! What's that supposed to mean, anyway?

Rafiki: It means you're a baboon . . . and I'm not.

Adult Simba: I think you're a little confused.

Rafiki: Wrong! I'm not the one who's confused. You don't even know who you are!

Adult Simba: Oh, and I suppose you know?

Rafiki: Sure do. You're Mufasa's boy!

Simba is finally convinced that, yes, he is the true king, and it's his responsibility to save the pride of lions from Scar and the hyenas. He rushes to the rescue and, with the help of his friends and all the other lions, succeeds in returning the pride lands to a lush, vibrant place that feeds everyone.

Does this movie remind you of *Hamlet*? Because it's meant for children, it does skip many of the deaths, but several of the plot points are similar. A man, or male lion, kills his brother to become king. The character of Simba, just like the character of Hamlet, hesitates to confront his uncle.

Simba is also visited by the ghost of his father, who exacts a promise, much in the same way Hamlet's father's ghost speaks to him.

Mufasa's Ghost: You have forgotten who you are and so have forgotten me. Look inside yourself, Simba. You are more than what you have become. You must take your place in the circle of life.

Adult Simba: How can I go back? I'm not who I used to be.

Mufasa's Ghost: Remember who you are. You are my son and the one true king. Remember who you are.

Adult Simba: No! Please! Don't leave me!

Mufasa's Ghost: Remember.

Adult Simba: Father!

Mufasa's Ghost: Remember.

Compare this to a section of Shakespeare's play, when King Hamlet's ghost begs his own son to remember his sworn revenge. While Mufasa is urging Simba to remember that he is the king and to be true to himself, Hamlet's ghost seems to be more selfish, urging Hamlet to remember him and his promise to kill Claudius.

King Hamlet's Ghost: Fare thee well at once!
The glow-worm shows the matin to be near,
And 'gins to pale his uneffectual fire:
Adieu, adieu! Hamlet, remember me.

(act 1 scene 5)

As King Hamlet's ghost says goodbye, he begs his son to remember him and the promise of revenge.

The first page of *Hamlet* in the First Folio, 1623

THE TRAGEDIE OF
HAMLET, Prince of Denmarke.

What was the real relationship between Hamlet and Ophelia? None of these questions are fully answered in the play, so contemporary writers make up their own answers.

FOLIO FACT

By telling her to "get thee to a nunnery," Hamlet is suggesting that Ophelia never have children so that they can't turn out to be bad.

BOOKS BASED ON *HAMLET*

One way authors create new work from the story of *Hamlet* is by telling the tale from the point of view of another character. Often, this character is Ophelia. In Shakespeare's *Hamlet*, Ophelia is frail and weak—she loses her tenuous grip on reality after her father is killed and her boyfriend seems to go mad. Eventually, the worsening order of events in Elsinore Castle drives her to drown herself.

We rarely get to see Hamlet and Ophelia together, which makes it very difficult to discern their actual relationship. Are they in love? In one of the few scenes they do share, they are hateful and hurtful to each other.

> **Ophelia:** Could beauty, my lord, have better commerce than with honesty?
>
> **Hamlet:** Ay, truly; for the power of beauty will sooner transform honesty from what it is to a bawd than the force of honesty can translate beauty into his likeness: this was sometime a paradox, but now the time gives it proof. I did love you once.
>
> **Ophelia:** Indeed, my lord, you made me believe so.
>
> **Hamlet:** You should not have believed me; for virtue cannot so inoculate our old stock but we shall relish of it: I loved you not.
>
> **Ophelia:** I was the more deceived.
>
> **Hamlet:** Get thee to a nunnery . . . .
>
> (act 3 scene 1)

What is Hamlet telling Ophelia in this scene? Does he think she's beautiful? Does he believe she's good?

He is saying that even though he might have made her believe that he loved her, she shouldn't assume he was telling the truth. He says this is because people are, at the core, dishonest, even when they try to be good.

The book *Ophelia* by Lisa Klein is told from the perspective of Ophelia herself. The story starts before King Hamlet has been killed. In this version of events, Hamlet and Ophelia are truly in love. They meet in secret and eventually marry without anyone knowing, except Hamlet's best friend, Horatio, who promises to remain loyal to them both. Does this plot remind you of another of Shakespeare's plays?

When King Hamlet dies and Gertrude and Claudius marry, Hamlet leaves Ophelia behind in a fit of mad rage against his family. It isn't long before she realizes she's pregnant.

Teenage pregnancy is a hard issue in any century, but in 1601 it meant utter desolation. Unmarried pregnant women of any age couldn't work, had no money, and often tried to hide their pregnancies from their families and neighbors. In Ophelia's case, she's desperate enough to fake her own death—by drowning, which parallels Ophelia's death by drowning in Shakespeare's *Hamlet*. She runs away to France, where she finds a convent of nuns willing to hide her and care for her. She does, in fact, get herself to a nunnery, and survives the tragedy of Hamlet.

Klein weaves quotes from Shakespeare's play into her own book, which makes the text connect well with the play. Also, her book feels authentic, and the sometimes flowery language lends a seventeenth-century quality to her writing.

JULIET AND OPHELIA

Sometimes, elements of other plays slip into stories based on particular works. In *Ophelia*, the main character's solution to the dual problem of her abandonment by Hamlet and her pregnancy is to fake her own death. Remember Juliet's solution to the problem of Romeo's banishment in *Romeo and Juliet*? Like Juliet, Ophelia takes a syrup of different herbs that put her into a deep sleep that resembles death and fools everyone into thinking she's gone. Ophelia's plan succeeds far better than Juliet's. While Juliet wakens only to kill herself after finding her beloved Romeo dead, Ophelia's plot works perfectly. She wakens in a healer's hut and escapes to France.

Yo, MC Hamlet!

Andrew Robert MacFarlane Nielsen, otherwise known as MC Lars, wrote a rap song based on *Hamlet* that follows the play fairly accurately, with a slight twist at the end. Instead of Horatio whispering, "Good night, sweet prince," to Hamlet, Hamlet says it to the memory of Ophelia.

If you're ever up in Denmark
on a moonlit night
You'll hear Ophelia's sad song
when the full moon's bright
Baby, I'm sorry I messed
up, good night my sweet
princess
May flights of angels
sing thee to thy rest.

You can listen to the song here.

🔍 MC Lars Hey There Ophelia

At that moment, our father stumbled into the room, waving his arms to hasten Laertes' departure. He flung out all his favored maxims as if strewing flowers after my brother.

"This above all, be true to yourself, and then you cannot be false to any man," he cried to Laertes' departing back.

This scene in *Ophelia* parallels act I scene 3 in *Hamlet*, in which Polonius offers advice to Laertes, including, "This above all: to thine own self be true." Why do you think Klein changed the wording slightly in her book, which is meant for audiences in the twenty-first century?

Another way authors weave stories from Shakespeare into their books is by introducing the plays to contemporary characters. Author Gary D. Schmidt does this in his novel, *The Wednesday Wars*. This book is set in the 1960s, when news reports about the Vietnam War dominated the television in most living rooms on Long Island, where 12-year-old Holling Hoodhood lives with his family.

Holling is something of an outsider—a familiar role in Shakespeare's plays—because he is the only Presbyterian in a class of mostly Jewish and Catholic kids. Every Wednesday, his classmates leave school for religious instruction while he stays behind with his teacher.

Mrs. Baker decides that Shakespeare will best serve these odd afternoons, and gives Holling an old collection of his plays. By May, they've gotten to *Hamlet*.

Holling is pretty distracted by his home life. His father is a successful architect and his mother never stands up to his father's insistence on complete control of the family.

Meanwhile, Holling's sister is becoming more active in speaking out against the Vietnam War, which makes his father very angry. After a big fight, the family gets very quiet around each other.

> Sort of like things between Claudius, Gertrude, and Hamlet. You can't say a lot if the whole time you're wondering if everyone else is really thinking about the thing you're not supposed to be thinking about, because you're afraid the thing you're not supposed to be thinking about is going to harrow you with fear and wonder. Or something like that.

Mrs. Baker helps Holling see the similarities between his situation and Hamlet's. Hamlet feels forced into a course of revenge because of the promise he made to his father's ghost, while Holling feels forced into a career as an architect because that's what his father has planned for him.

> "But you want to decide for yourself," said Mrs. Baker.
> I nodded. I wanted to decide for myself.
> "And you're afraid," said Mrs. Baker, "that you won't get the chance."
> "That I won't get the chance to see what I can do with the slings and arrows of outrageous fortune," I said.

FOLIO FACT

Author Gary D. Schmidt had the same experience as his character, Holling, when he was growing up as the only Presbyterian in a neighborhood of Jewish and Catholic people.

Write down what you think each word means: **timeless**, **paralyzing**, **passive**, **motto**, **tenuous**, **interspersed**, **prop**, **dominate**, and **collaborator**.

Compare your definitions with those of your friends or classmates. Did you all come up with the same meanings? Turn to the text and glossary if you need help.

What soliloquy by Hamlet does this remind you of? "To be or not to be—that is the question: whether 'tis nobler in the mind to suffer the slings and arrows of outrageous fortune or to take arms against a sea of troubles, and by opposing end them."

Though Hamlet is considering whether it's better to be dead or alive and Holling is thinking about whether it's better to do what your father tells you or not, their approaches to the different problems are the same. How else are Hamlet and Holling similar characters? How are they different?

> Just as Shakespeare was inspired by the tale of Amleth and other tales of faked madness, many artists and writers are inspired by *Hamlet*.

Its enduring themes of revenge, self-doubt, and mortality are rich fields in which to cultivate new art. Can you think of any popular culture you've experienced that relates to *Hamlet*?

KEY QUESTIONS

- How did Mufasa and King Hamlet treat their sons differently? Why?
- Many great works of literature are about characters who feel like outsiders. Why are people who don't fit in interesting to audiences and readers?

DESIGN THE PLAY-WITHIN-THE-PLAY

An important moment in *Hamlet* is when the cast of characters watches the play that Hamlet has arranged to be performed at the castle. He secretly organized the players into a plot of his own devising, one that reflects his suspicions of how his father was murdered. He reasons that Claudius will react with guilt if the play tells the truth of what happened. And it works!

- **Choose a book or movie or song that you are already familiar with.** Pay attention to the different subplots and themes that are part of the work.

- **Identify a problem in the work that the characters are trying to solve.** For example, Harry Potter wanted to keep his friends safe from evil wizards.

- **Write a version of a play-within-a-play for your chosen piece.** How might your characters use other characters to try and solve the problem? How could they reframe the conflict in a way that helps them work through the details? Harry Potter might have arranged the ghosts of Hogwarts into the same type of problems he was having to better understand how to defeat Voldemort.

> To investigate more, look out for more plays-within-plays or stories-within-stories when reading works by Shakespeare. Why do you think authors appreciate this literary device? What does it add to a piece of literature?

FOLIO FACT

A play-within-a-play is a literary device called *mise en abyme*, which is French for "into the abyss." Why do you think this definition fits this device? This term is also used to describe the feeling people sometimes get when they stand between two mirrors that reflect back at each other for infinity. How is this similar to a play-within-a-play?

Chapter Five

Twelfth Night

YOU ARE MY TWIN SISTER!?! WE SHOULD TOTALLY SWITCH PLACES AND GET OUR PARENTS BACK TOGETHER!

Why is a plot twist involving twins being mistaken for each other so much fun in any century?

Audiences love to witness stories of mistaken identities. Perhaps these tales appeal to the human desire to be someone else, if only for a little while!

There's a long history of men and women dressing up as the other gender to do something they otherwise wouldn't be able to do. During war time, many women disguise themselves as men so they can go to the battlefield and fight for their countries. Men have often dressed as women to play parts in plays when women weren't allowed on stage. Women have also hidden in men's clothes when traveling, because thieves are less likely to attack a man than a woman.

In *Twelfth Night*, a young woman named Viola dresses as a man to get herself a job. The hilarity that follows is the stuff that makes this play a comedy, one of Shakespeare's finest.

Even though *Twelfth Night* is a comedy, it harbors dark undertones. A subplot portrays what happens when a practical joke goes too far. This subplot ends ominously, with a threat that casts a shadow over the happy ending. Why do you think Shakespeare added a bitter section to an otherwise funny play? Do you think he was making an observation about human nature?

THE STORY

The play might not seem like a comedy at first. The first character we meet is Orsino, the duke of a kingdom on the Adriatic Sea called Illyria. Orsino pines away with love for Olivia, a rich woman in the kingdom. He complains of his problems to his attendants.

> If music be the food of love, play on;
> Give me excess of it, that, surfeiting,
> the appetite may sicken, and so die . . . .
>
> (act 1 scene 1)

When Orsino says this, he is hoping that by listening to music he will finally be made sick of love and his desire for Olivia will dissipate.

Unfortunately for Orsino, Olivia has no interest in suitors. Her brother died recently, and Olivia has sworn to wear a veil for seven years. She refuses to meet with any men during this time. Orsino is heartsick that the woman he loves won't even let him look at her.

Meanwhile, a shipwreck casts a young woman named Viola on Illyria's shores. Though she is grateful to be alive, she is also devastated that her twin brother, Sebastian, did not survive the shipwreck. She decides to dress as a boy so she can go to work for the duke. She figures this is her best chance to assure her safety and livelihood. She cuts her hair, flattens her chest with bandages, and calls herself Cesario. She is quickly accepted into Orsino's entourage.

Orsino enjoys Cesario's company and the two become friends. He decides that Cesario has a better chance at getting Olivia to listen to Orsino's pleas of love and sends him (her) to woo her. Olivia accepts his visit, but is suspicious and hides behind her veil.

Orsino's quote is a famous one: **"If music be the food of love, play on."** People tend to think it means that if music is like love, they want more of it because it feels good. Orsino, however, equates over-listening to music to overeating so much that you don't want to eat anymore. He doesn't want to feel love anymore.

FOLIO FACT

Illyria was a real place, located along the Adriatic Sea on the Balkan Peninsula. In Shakespeare's time, not many people in England knew about this country, which let Shakespeare use it how he wanted without having to worry about facts.

By the end of Viola's visit, though, Olivia has been charmed. Not by the thought of Orsino—it's Viola dressed as Cesario that she finds attractive. She thinks to herself, "Thy tongue, the face, thy limbs, actions, and spirit / Do give thee fivefold blazon." A blazon is a coat of arms. She is saying here that she can tell Viola is from a good family just by looking at her.

The first page of *Twelfth Night* in the First Folio, 1623

> "I cannot love him," she says to Cesario, talking about Orsino. "Let him send no more—unless perchance you come to me again / To tell me how he takes it."

Viola, still dressed as Cesario, has a problem beyond the fact that the woman her master loves has fallen in love with her. Viola finds herself in love with Orsino. She can't tell him, because that would reveal her gender and she'd be sure to lose her job and the chance to be near Orsino. The situation torments her, as the following scene shows.

Duke Orsino: How dost thou like this tune?

Viola: It gives a very echo to the seat
Where Love is throned.

Duke Orsino: Thou dost speak masterly:
My life upon't, young though thou art, thine eye
Hath stay'd upon some favour that it loves:
Hath it not, boy?

Viola: A little, by your favour.

Duke Orsino: What kind of woman is't?

Viola: Of your complexion.

Duke Orsino: She is not worth thee, then. What years, i' faith?

Viola: About your years, my lord.

(act 2 scene 4)

What is happening in this scene? What is Viola revealing to the audience?

Shakespeare has set up a love triangle between Orsino, Olivia, and Viola/Cesario. Audiences find this funny, because they know Viola's true identity and it's a delight watching the other characters say things to her, thinking she's a man.

Duke Orsino is not Olivia's only suitor. A man named Sir Andrew is also vying for her affections. Sir Andrew is a comical figure in the play—he has a big ego but a small vocabulary and often finds himself confused about what's going on around him. He joins Toby, Olivia's uncle, and Maria, Olivia's maid, in developing a practical joke on a servant named Malvolio, who also hopes to win Olivia's love.

The pranksters write a letter in Olivia's handwriting professing love for Malvolio and listing a few things she wishes he would do for her: "Remember who commended thy yellow stockings and wished to see thee ever cross-gartered." They drop the letter in the garden, where Malvolio finds it and thinks it's from his lady, professing her love for him.

Meanwhile, the audience is shown that Viola's twin brother, Sebastian, is alive. He was rescued by a sailor named Antonio, who accompanies him to Illyria, even though Antonio fought against Illyrian soldiers and his life is in danger if he's spotted in the area.

[
Sebastian believes his sister is dead, just as she believes he is dead. Only the audience knows the truth.
]

FOLIO FACT

Olivia's Uncle Toby hopes Sir Andrew will win Olivia's love because Sir Andrew is rich while Toby is not. Uncle Toby hopes to increase the income of the house with Sir Andrew's fortune.

Garters are strips of material that hold up stockings. Men used to wear them in Shakespeare's time.

This knowledge sets up a sense of foreshadowing. The audience knows there are two characters who look very similar roaming the same town, and the chances of them being mistaken for each other by their respective friends is great.

Foreshadowing is a useful literary technique. It makes the audience feel anticipation about events to come, which adds to the dramatic tension within the play.

Before the fun of mistaken identity can start, however, Malvolio finds himself playing the fool. When Olivia calls her servant to her room, she's shocked to see him wearing yellow stockings and crossed garters, and even more shocked when he acts familiar with her, as though they were in love with each other. Olivia decides he must be mad and puts him into Toby's care. Toby takes the practical joke too far and locks Malvolio up in a dark room as treatment for a madness that doesn't actually exist.

Sebastian, meanwhile, manages to make his way to Olivia's castle, where people mistake him for Cesario. Feste, Olivia's fool, is the first to encounter the twin.

> Well held out, i' faith! No, I do not know you; nor I am not sent to you by my lady, to bid you come speak with her; nor your name is not Master Cesario; nor this is not my nose neither. Nothing that is so is so.
>
> (act 4 scene 1)

Feste, though he's the fool, is wise enough to realize that nothing is as it seems.

ORIGINS OF *TWELFTH NIGHT*

Just as with many of Shakespeare's other plays, *Twelfth Night* is not solely a work of Shakespeare's imagination. He was probably inspired by a story called "Apolonius and Silla" that was included in Barnabe Riche's *Riche his Farewell to Militarie Profession conteining verie pleasaunt discourses fit for a peaceable tyme*, which was published in 1581. Riche was a soldier about 24 years older than Shakespeare. He published his book after he retired from the army.

Riche's stories weren't wholly original, either. Remember, back then, writers were comfortable borrowing from each other's work. Riche was likely influenced by an Italian play called *Gl'Ingannati*, which translates to *The Deceived Ones*. This play was written by a group of people who were part of the Accademia degli Intronati, a gathering place for intellectual aristocrats in the Italian city of Siena.

Twelfth Night is another example of Shakespeare taking inspiration from other works and from society around him. How has this play inspired writers and movie makers of today? We'll find out in the next chapter.

Scholars believe that Shakespeare read *Gl'Ingannati* l as Riche's story.

AB LAB

te down what you
each word means:
lertone, **ominous**,
ipate, **entourage**,
torment, **garters**,
cial commentary,
elry, and **riotous**.

Compare your
nitions with those
of your friends or
assmates. Did you
come up with the
he meanings? Turn
e text and glossary
if you need help.

KEY QUESTIONS

- Why do you think Shakespeare mixes the hilarity of a comedy with the danger of a prank gone bad?
- Why are so many of Shakespeare's plays about love and its complications?
- How do you think seeing a play acted out is different from reading the play?

When Olivia meets Sebastian, she thinks it's the man she loves standing before her and invites him into her house. Sebastian is pleased by this particular confusing moment, because upon seeing Olivia, he falls in love with her. Olivia is thrilled that the object of her affections has finally come around to loving her in return, and they marry each other at once.

> Only the audience knows Sebastian's true identity and the grand mistake that Olivia has just made.

Orsino and his entourage, including Cesario, arrive at Olivia's castle. Olivia comes to greet them and Orsino confronts her, saying he might have to hurt Cesario because Olivia wouldn't return his love. When Cesario sides with Orsino and prepares to leave with him, Olivia protests, because, after all, this is her new husband. Everyone is even more confused when Sir Andrew and Sir Toby come to the courtyard and announce that Cesario injured them in a sword fight. Huh?

For Shakespeare, even comedy was an opportunity to explore human struggle. While the main story focuses on the love triangle and the funny aspects of a woman dressing as a man, the subplot of Malvolio's takedown is an interesting look into the darker side of jokes.

Finally, Sebastian arrives, the twins each discover that the other survived the shipwreck, and the couples are sorted out according to emotional attachment. Olivia and Sebastian together, Viola and Orsino together.

All might seem to be ending in merriment, but then Malvolio appears, accusing his lady, Olivia, of doing him great harm. He shows her the letter, which she explains she did not write, but he won't be satisfied. He vows, "I'll be revenged on the whole pack of you!"

The final moment of the play is granted to Feste, the fool, who ends it with a song, the first and last stanzas of which go like this:

> When that I was and a little tiny boy,
> With hey, ho, the wind and the rain,
> A foolish thing was but a toy,
> For the rain it raineth every day.
>
> A great while ago the world begun,
> With hey, ho, the wind and the rain,
> But that's all one, our play is done,
> And we'll strive to please you every day.
>
> (act 5 scene 1)

What do you think this song means? It's a confusing end to a sometimes confusing play. Is Shakespeare reminding his audience that despite the happy ending they've just witnessed, storms happen frequently and happiness is always temporary? Is he encouraging people to take the long view and remember that the world is large, life is long, and there are always more chances for happiness? This is a topic scholars have debated since the play was first performed. What do you think?

THEMES IN *TWELFTH NIGHT*

Twelfth Night is the only one of Shakespeare's plays that has two titles—*Twelfth Night* and *What You Will*. From the very first page, this is a play of doubles. Two brothers lost, two people in love, another two people in love, and then another two people in love!

There are two opposing strands of social commentary running through *Twelfth Night*. Social commentary is when a work of literature expresses an opinion on what is happening in society. In *Twelfth Night*, the scowling character of Malvolio frowns on all aspects of joy and revelry, believing that Sir Toby, Sir Andrew, and their friends shouldn't be having so much fun.

Opposing Malvolio are the characters of Sir Toby, Sir Andrew, and pretty much every other character. They are all willing to take part in the riotous nature of love, joy, anger—the full spectrum of human emotion. Do you think any of this dynamic exists in society today? Are there some groups that believe that life should always be taken seriously and others that believe in the value of fun and parties?

CHOOSE YOUR OWN ADVENTURE

There are a lot of chances for fate to interfere in *Twelfth Night*. What if Sebastian hadn't survived the shipwreck? What if Olivia had decided she loved Orsino after all? What if Malvolio hadn't been pranked? Read the summary of the play over again. Then devise a game to explore the plot twists that might have been.

- **Create a game board out of a map of the world of Illyria.** Draw and color the houses, trails, and village where the action takes place. Where is Duke Orsino's residence compared to Olivia's residence? What is the path that Cesario has to travel to get to Olivia's estate? Where is the shore where the survivors of the shipwreck wash up?

- **Create game pieces for each character.** For example, you could use a quarter to represent Olivia, since she is wealthy.

- **Ask a group of friends to imagine the scene when Cesario first visits Olivia.** Act out the scene on the game board with the game pieces.

- **Now change the scene.** Make different choices for your characters and see how the story unfolds. Does each character still end up with the same person as in the play? Do any new conflicts arise? Can you make the storyline more exciting or more adventurous?

To investigate more, introduce new characters into your role-playing game. Maybe Olivia has a sister or Duke Orsino has a mother who dislikes Orsino's love interests. What can you learn about the characters by having them interact with new people?

READ THE PLAY

You can read the whole *Twelfth Night* play at this website. A great way to read one of Shakespeare's plays is to do it with a group and have everyone act out a part. Pay attention to the major plot changes, such as when Olivia falls in love with Cesario.

 Twelfth Night MIT

Chapter Six

Twelfth Night Today

How has *Twelfth Night* been used in popular culture to explore issues that affect people today?

Dressing as the opposite gender is a common phenomenon throughout history, because many opportunities weren't available to women and they had to hide their gender in order to succeed at certain things.

Girls dressed as boys, boys dressed as girls, and the confusion that can result are popular motifs in contemporary movies and books. Maybe because relationships can already be very confusing, people enjoy watching that confusion multiply as a result of mistaken identity! This type of plot also offers a chance for viewers and readers to think about the differences between men and women and to reflect on why these differences have often been the basis for discrimination.

It might seem strange to explore such complicated topics through comedy. Aren't funny movies and books supposed to be entertaining? They are, but humor can also be used as an opportunity to approach tough topics in a way that might be less intimidating than a serious discussion.

Think of the comedies you've read or seen. Are there ever serious moments contained within the jokes?

SHE'S THE MAN

This is a funny movie about what happens when a girl dresses as her twin brother to attend a boarding school. Through all the hilarious lines and delicious tensions, however, runs a very serious topic. Viola only chooses to go through with passing as a boy because her girls' soccer team was cut due to lack of funds, and the girls are prohibited from playing on the boys' team. Do you think this is fair?

When Viola and her teammates show up to soccer practice on the first day of school, they realize that their team has been cut because there isn't enough money to support both a boys' team and a girls' team. This is more than disappointing—the girls were hoping to attract the attention of college scouts to increase the possibility of scholarships. Unfortunately, they're not allowed to play on the boys' team and complaining about it gets them nowhere.

Viola has a better idea, although it's a complicated one. Her twin brother, Sebastian, is scheduled to start at his new boarding school, called Illyria, but he leaves town to spend a few weeks in London, telling no one but Viola. Their parents are divorced and seem to be completely out of touch with the world.

> This makes it easy for Viola to find a wig, dress as a boy, and show up at Illyria to take her brother's place in his dorm room, classrooms, and on the soccer team.

SHE'S THE MAN

This movie is rated PG-13 by the MPAA for some sexual material.

Flawless plan, right? Except that Viola, dressed as Sebastian, falls for her roommate, who is named Duke Orsino. And Duke is interested in a girl called Olivia, who becomes "Sebastian's" lab partner and starts to fall for "him," since he's sensitive to the whims and needs of the female species (because he is one!).

> The love triangle is exactly the same
> as it was in Shakespeare's play—
> even the names are the same.

What makes this even harder on Viola is her mother's reminder that both she and her brother had promised to help out at the Junior League Carnival, an outdoor festival with rides and games. This makes for a stressful day of changing back and forth to satisfy everyone's expectations. Part of Viola's job is working the kissing booth, where Duke ends up kissing her.

When Sebastian returns from London, everything gets thrown into confusion, just as it does in *Twelfth Night* when Shakespeare's Sebastian returns from the presumed dead. Olivia is the first to come across the real Sebastian and without even speaking, gives him a kiss. Duke sees this exchange, and accuses his roommate of betraying him by kissing the girl he likes.

When Viola oversleeps and is late to the big soccer game against her old school the next day, Sebastian is sent onto the field in her place, because everyone thinks that he's the guy who's been playing with the team the whole season. Unfortunately, Sebastian stinks at soccer.

Viola gets to the game late and hides under the bleachers. She manages to nab her brother at halftime and explains the whole thing—they switch clothes so she can play the second half.

TITLE IX

In the real world, the premise of *She's the Man* doesn't exist. A law called Title IX states, "No person in the United States shall, on the basis of sex, be excluded from participation in, be denied the benefits of, or be subjected to discrimination under any education program or activity receiving federal financial assistance."

This means that schools that receive money from the federal government have to provide the same sports opportunities for girls as for boys. That means, if there's a boys' soccer team, there has to be a girls' soccer team, and if there's only enough money for one team, both boys and girls have to be allowed to play on it.

When Duke, who is still angry at "Sebastian" for kissing Olivia, refuses to pass "him" the ball, Viola stops play to explain to him that she's been impersonating her brother so she could play soccer. The Illyria coach calls out the other soccer coach for sexism, and the game goes on, with Viola making the winning goal for Illyria. However, she's not as thrilled about it as she'd like to be, because Duke is still mad at her.

Just as in Shakespeare's play, however, everything turns out all right in the end. The people who like each other end up with each other and everyone is happy. In *She's the Man*, there isn't even a character to cast a shadow over the joy with threats of revenge. Happily ever after is achieved when Viola and Duke share this scene.

Viola: So, what brings you here?

Duke: Well, a few days ago I kissed this girl at a kissing booth. And now, I just can't seem to stop thinking about it.

Viola: Neither can she.

Duke: Plus, I miss my roommate. I really liked him.

Viola: Well, he's right in here.
[pointing to her heart]

Viola: Listen, I know I should have told you who I was, but I was afraid. I'm sorry.

Duke: Well, you know maybe if I had known you were a girl, we wouldn't have talked like we did, and got to know each other the same way. And that would've been a shame.

Viola: Just so you know, everything you told me when I was a guy, just made me like you so much more as a girl.

Duke: Ok, but just from here on in, everything would just be a lot easier if you stayed a girl.

MOTOCROSS

Another movie that is based on *Twelfth Night* is called *Motocross*. In this movie, a girl named Andrea dresses as a boy and enters a motorbike race when her twin brother, Andrew, hurts his leg and can't ride. She proves to her father that she is as good a racer as any boy. This is another example of sports being used as a way to challenge stereotypes of boys and girls and how they play.

Andrew: Guys would do anything to beat you.

Andrea: Yeah, but they'd have to keep up with me first.

This movie outlines an example of sexism and offers a funny resolution to a hard problem. While it's unlikely that anyone would ever solve the problem of unfair treatment the way Viola did, the movie offers a chance for viewers to explore the absurdity of the idea that men deserve a soccer team more than women.

In a scene from *Twelfth Night*, Orsino claims to Cesario that women couldn't possibly love in the same capacity as men.

> **Duke Orsino:** There is no woman's sides
> Can bide the beating of so strong a passion
> As love doth give my heart; no woman's heart
> So big, to hold so much; they lack retention . . . .

(act 2 scene 4)

Orsino is saying that women aren't physically capable of loving as much as he loves. Shakespeare's Viola counters with a story about a sister who loved as much as Orsino loves and the trauma it caused her. While the movie version of Viola isn't told she can't love as well as men, she is told she can't play soccer because the boys' team is more important. It takes a gigantic effort for her to be allowed to play soccer.

FOLIO FACT

One of the boys at the boarding school is a troublemaker named Malcolm, who has a pet tarantula named Malvolio.

PERHAPS I CAN HELP! I HAPPEN TO BE A WOMAN AND CAN GIVE YOU SOME TIPS!

FANTASTIC IDEA, ELIZA! SHARE YOUR WISDOM WITH OUR MATTHEW.

MASTER RICKY AND I WILL SEARCH HIGH AND LOW FOR MY SCRIPT!

> Instead of proving herself on the field of love, Viola has to prove herself on the soccer field.

By using an ancient plot twist, the makers of *She's the Man* use comedy to reveal the painful truth of sexism in a way viewers might find accessible, since it's mixed with funny entertainment. Do you think that serious topics are served better by comedy or serious works of art? Why?

THE FOOL'S GIRL

Writer Celia Rees uses her book, *The Fool's Girl*, to explore the darker shades of revenge that are hinted at in Shakespeare's play. Rees uses characters from Shakespeare's *Twelfth Night*, plus the character of Shakespeare himself, plus her own imagined characters to create a tapestry of past and present.

When readers first meet Violetta, her hometown of Illyria is in ruins and she is alive only because of the daring tricks of her friend, Feste, the fool of her mother's old friend. The two of them are earning money as street performers on the streets of London when William Shakespeare, the playwright, happens upon them. He's fascinated with them and recognizes Feste as a master fool. During dinner, Violetta tells some of her story to him.

Violetta's mother was Viola, who washed up on the shores of Illyria after a shipwreck and dressed as a man to work for Duke Orsino. The story follows the same path as the original play, with happy endings in the form of two weddings and the eventual birth of two children, Violetta to Viola and Orsino, and Stephano to Olivia and Sebastian.

Sadly, Malvolio's vow of revenge comes to fruition and destroys not only the happiness of the people at fault for his mistreatment, but the entire country. Sebastian never quite accepts his wife's friendship with his twin sister, and when Viola goes missing, a pile of clothes at the edge of the sea is the only clue—people assume she drowned herself. The kingdom splits apart further because the Duke and Olivia retreat into their own personal sorrow and neglect the kingdom.

Sebastian's bitterness turns to mutiny as he sides with Illyria's enemy, Venice, and attacks the remaining forces of Illyria. He takes control, with help from Malvolio and Sir Andrew, who has shed his bumbling persona for a much more conniving one. The children and Feste, Violetta's faithful companion, are sent away as prisoners.

However, Feste is a master of escape and manages to free himself, track down Violetta, and free her. Once in England, they gain the trust and help of William Shakespeare. Violetta wants to regain an icon that Malvolio stole from Illyria, a figure that she believes is necessary to return Illyria to its once promising state. First, they must help foil plans of a conspiracy against the queen and dodge the many spies Malvolio has sent to capture them.

The Fool's Girl is thick with references to Shakespeare, not only to *Twelfth Night* but also to *Romeo and Juliet*, *A Midsummer Night's Dream*, *Hamlet*, and many more. For example, does the following passage seem familiar?

> He had been staring at a skull, clotted with earth, mossy with clumps of hair still attached here and there, smelling of the grave. The recently disinterred, dug up to make way for a fresh occupant, as often happened in the burying grounds of London.

Do you remember the scene in *Hamlet* when Hamlet pauses in a graveyard and holds up a skull to examine it and discovers it belonged to someone he once knew? The two scenes are directly related to each other.

> Alas, poor Yorick! I knew him, Horatio: a fellow of infinite jest, of most excellent fancy: he hath borne me on his back a thousand times; and now, how abhorred in my imagination it is! my gorge rims at it. Here hung those lips that I have kissed I know not how oft.

(act 5 scene 1)

Why do you think Rees titled her novel, *The Fool's Girl?*

FOLIO FACT

A new series of Shakespeare's plays, called OMG Shakespeare, are written in texting language. Titles include *srsly Hamlet*, *YOLO Juliet*, and *Macbeth #killingit*.

KEY QUESTIONS

- **Why is it important to confront discrimination instead of simply ignore it?**

- **Why do sports present a good opportunity to explore what discrimination means and how it affects people?**

- **Should there be rules for including a real figure as a character in a book, as Rees does with Shakespeare?**

> Celia Rees weaves glimmers of Shakespeare's plays into her own book, which sends readers on a kind of treasure hunt as they make their way through the plot.

The book also plays with the setting, events, and people of Shakespeare's real life—we meet his wife, Anne, and his daughters and see the home he buys and renovates in Stratford, called New Place. We even slip inside his point of view as he feels grief for his dead son, Hamnet.

> He felt a chill of his own as boys left off fishing and messing on the bank and came to run alongside them, attracted by the painted wagon. He aught himself looking for his own lad, Hamnet, among them, although he'd have been too old to play by the river. He was eleven when he was taken by a sudden fever.

How is this passage, told through the character Shakespeare's perspective, different from a paragraph in a history book about the boy's death? Why is it sometimes useful to fictionalize history? Is it ever a dangerous thing to do? Why?

There are many movies and books that involved girls and boys dressing as the opposite gender, and not all of them are based on Shakespeare. However, by using the scaffolding of the plot of *Twelfth Night*, writers can explore what it means to have to pretend to be someone you're not in order to get a fair chance. Can you think of other stories that reflect the plot of *Twelfth Night*?

R U OK?

What do you think Shakespeare's opinion of smartphones would be if he were alive today? Scholars think Shakespeare was interested in new inventions and ideas, so maybe he would have liked having a tiny computer he could carry around in his pocket. What would his plays have been like if he'd been used to texting?

- **Rewrite parts of *Twelfth Night* as if you were one of the characters texting with another character.** For example, what kind of texts would Viola, dressed as Cesario, send to Orsino? You can write your texts out on paper or type them on a device.

- **Text back to the first character as the second character.** How do you use texting language and emojis to express the personality of the character?

> To investigate more, rewrite great soliloquies from *Romeo and Juliet* and *Hamlet*. How can you reach the emotional depths of these speeches with texting? Does the structure of the language you use change the meaning of the lines?

VOCAB LAB

Write down what you think each word means: **motif, discrimination, impersonate, sexism, absurdity, persona, conniving, foil,** and **conspiracy**.

Compare your definitions with those of your friends or classmates. Did you all come up with the same meanings? Turn to the text and glossary if you need help.

Chapter Seven

A Midsummer Night's Dream

HEE-HEE! HIS ONLINE PROFILE IS PERFECT! NOW TO FIND A MATCH...

Why does a dream-like story about fairies interfering with the love lives of humans hold so much interest for audiences?

Shakespeare captures the idea that love can be a very dreamy state, a concept that modern-day humans recognize as well as people did in the Elizabethan Age.

In *A Midsummer Night's Dream*, Shakespeare addresses the very nature of plays and what they offer. At the end of the play, the character of Robin Goodfellow, or Puck as he's better known, addresses the audience directly and advises them to think of the play as a kind of dream. Why would Puck recommend viewing the play as a dream? What is similar about plays and dreams?

The four humans in the story are subject to the whims of love. Is love always a straight and steady experience? Once you fall in love, do you stay in love with the same person, forever? Shakespeare addresses these questions by placing his human characters into bizarre situations caused by the whims and mistakes of the fairies.

THE STORY

A Midsummer Night's Dream takes place in Athens, Greece, and contains three intertwined subplots. Two groups of humans and one group of fairies encounter each other in the woods during the course of a few nights.

> Through the relationships that form and break as a result of these encounters with the fairies, Shakespeare explores what it means to love.

The play begins with Theseus, the Duke of Athens, and Hippolyta, the Amazon queen who was recently defeated by Theseus and brought back to Greece. They are discussing their wedding, which is to happen in four days' time. Hippolyta says to her fiancé:

> Four days will quickly steep themselves in night;
> Four nights will quickly dream away the time;
> And then the moon, like to a silver bow
> New-bent in heaven, shall behold the night
> Of our solemnities.

(act 1 scene 1)

What is Hippolyta saying with these lines? Already, the trope, or thematic phrase, of dream is introduced into the play.

While the two are talking, a man named Egeus comes to complain to the duke that his daughter, Hermia, is being disobedient. Hermia is in love with Lysander, but Demetrius is in love with her, and it's Demetrius that Egeus wants her to marry. To make things more complicated, Hermia's friend, Helena, is in love with Demetrius. Shakespeare immediately makes things confusing for his audience!

Hermia and Lysander decide to run away to avoid Hermia's marriage to Demetrius. Hermia confides her plans to her friend, Helena, who tells Demetrius about the couple's plan to meet the next night in the forest. He follows them to try to stop them from running away together, and Helena follows Demetrius.

Hippolyta seems eager for her wedding, even though the violent circumstances of how she got to Greece would probably be distracting for someone in real life.

FOLIO FACT

According to Greek law, Hermia must comply with her father's wishes or risk a harsh punishment, even death.

The local tradesmen are very funny, bumbling characters who don't quite realize they look like fools trying to rehearse a play together.

Meanwhile, a group of local tradesmen decides to rehearse a play in the hopes of performing it at the wedding of Theseus and Hippolyta. The king and queen of fairies are also out and about in the woods. They're having a dispute over who has jurisdiction over a human changeling—King Oberon wants the boy in his camp, but Queen Titania has taken a liking to the boy because she knew his mother.

Oberon decides to trick Titania into giving up the child. He orders Puck to find a certain flower that causes people to fall in love with the first person they see upon waking.

[Oberon figures that he'll distract Titania by making her fall in love and then he can take the child.]

Oberon witnesses Helena pleading with Demetrius to love her, and decides that Demetrius, too, could use some of the love potion so that he will fall in love with poor Helena. Puck gets the potion, gives it to Oberon to paint onto Titania's sleeping lids, finds the Athenian he thinks is Demetrius and applies the potion—but it's actually Lysander. Lysander wakes and falls in love with Helena.

FOLIO FACT

Astronomer William Herschel named Uranus's two largest moons, Oberon and Titania, in 1787 after the fairy king and queen.

Meanwhile, Puck finds the actors and decides to play a trick on the man named Bottom. He changes Bottom's head into the head of an ass, or a donkey. Titania, sleeping nearby, wakes up, sees Bottom, and falls in love with him, donkey head and all.

When Oberon overhears Hermia and Demetrius arguing about Lysander, he figures out that Puck has enchanted the wrong man. Oberon applies the potion to Demetrius so he will wake up and fall in love with Helena.

[
Helena, Demetrius, Lysander, and Hermia
all argue about who loves whom.
]

Oberon tries to fix all of the mistakes. He sends Puck to remove the love spell from Lysander so that he'll go back to loving Hermia.

Meanwhile, Titania has forgotten all about the child she wanted to keep from Oberon. She's head-over-heels in love with Bottom. When Oberon removes the spell from Titania, she feels as if it has all been a dream. Bottom feels the same way when Puck puts his head back to rights.

> I have had a most rare vision. I have had a dream, past the wit of man to say what dream it was: man is but an ass, if he go about to expound this dream. Methought I was—there is no man can tell what. Methought I was,—and methought I had,—but man is but a patched fool, if he will offer to say what methought I had. The eye of man hath not heard, the ear of man hath not seen, man's hand is not able to taste, his tongue to conceive, nor his heart to report, what my dream was.

(act 4 scene 1)

The four Athenians are found in the woods by Theseus and his entourage. They try to explain what happened during the last couple of nights, but they're all confused about the exact events. However, they are all sure about who they love, so Theseus announces that instead of one marriage, they will have three!

At the wedding, the group of players finally gets to perform its play, and it's a bit of a mess. The audience can't help but comment throughout it.

The play is *Pyramus and Thisbe*, the story of two people who love each other but are separated by a wall. When they do manage to set a time and place to meet, it becomes a tragedy. Thisbe arrives first but is scared away by a lion, and leaves her cloak stained with blood. When Pyramus finds the cloak, he thinks Thisbe has been killed and stabs himself to death. Thisbe comes back and sees her beloved dead, and kills herself with his dagger.

FOLIO FACT

Does this play-within-a-play remind you of another Shakespeare play?

The four lovers from a 1935 movie version of *A Midsummer Night's Dream*

A Midsummer Night's Dream ends with Puck's monologue about dreams.

> And this weak and idle theme,
> No more yielding but a dream,
> Gentles, do not reprehend:
> if you pardon, we will mend:
> And, as I am an honest Puck,
> If we have unearned luck
> Now to 'scape the serpent's tongue,
> We will make amends ere long;
> Else the Puck a liar call;
> So, good night unto you all.

(act 5 scene 1)

Why is he asking the audience to imagine that the play was all a dream? Puck isn't addressing the audience in character—he has stepped out of character and is speaking as an actor. Why do you think Shakespeare included this scene? Can you think of any contemporary performances that reveal the plot as a dream?

THEMES

Like many of Shakespeare's plays, *A Midsummer Night's Dream* is about love. It also reflects on the nature of dreams versus reality, and explores how the dream of love can be quite different from the reality of love. Through a series of dream-like experiences, the four young humans in the play are subjected to heartbreak and confusion before they are finally ready to be married to their true loves.

Dreams work as metaphors throughout the play. Being in love is described as being in a dream, while marriage, which is a more lasting kind of love, happens after waking from the dream. The act of watching a play is acknowledged as being a kind of dream, and the end of the play is the waking from the dream.

RHYMING COUPLETS

A Midsummer Night's Dream is perhaps Shakespeare's most lyrical play. The four young people in love with each other often speak in rhyming couplets. Even when Hermia and Helena are speaking with each other and despairing over their respective circumstances, they speak in a woven way.

Hermia: I frown upon him, yet he loves me still.

Helena: O that your frowns would teach my smiles such skill!

Hermia: I give him curses, yet he gives me love.

Helena: O that my prayers could such affection move!

Hermia: The more I hate, the more he follows me.

Helena: The more I love, the more he hateth me.

Hermia: His folly, Helena, is no fault of mine.

Helena: None, but your beauty: would that fault were mine!

ORIGINS

In *A Midsummer Night's Dream*, Shakespeare doesn't draw from one specific source, though scholars have discovered common threads in other works. The most prominent of these is Geoffrey Chaucer's "A Knight's Tale," which is found in his *Canterbury Tales*.

In "A Knight's Tale," Chaucer tells the story of Theseus, the Duke of Athens, who discovers two men fighting each other over the love of a woman named Emily, who is the sister of Theseus's wife, Ypolita. Chaucer's Theseus makes an attempt to decide the fate of the two men and the woman. The men are to amass their own armies and fight in a tournament. The winner will take the woman's hand in marriage.

While Chaucer's story does not contain any fairies or love potions, it does have a few common themes and characters. Theseus appears in his role as leader, and two men are in love with one woman, as happens during the plot of Shakespeare's play. There are also allusions to the month of May, which is when *A Midsummer Night's Dream* takes place.

FOLIO FACT

Shakespeare collaborated with a writer named John Fletcher on a play called *The Two Noble Kinsmen* that also uses elements of Chaucer's "A Knight's Tale."

The plot of the play-within-the-play was also well known before Shakespeare. The story of Pyramus and Thisbe, the two lovers who are kept apart by a wall and whose romance ends tragically, was written about by the famous writer Ovid in his book, *Metamorphoses*. Ovid describes the scene where Pyramus discovers his love's bloodstained scarf:

> . . . he cries, "Two lovers will be lost in one night. She was the more deserving of a long life. I am the guilty spirit. I have killed you, poor girl, who told you to come by night to this place filled with danger, and did not reach it first. O, all you lions, that live amongst these rocks, tear my body to pieces, and devour my sinful flesh in your fierce jaws! Though it is cowardly to ask for death."

In Shakespeare's play-within-a-play, the bumbling actor, Bottom, overplays the part of Pyramus with gusto. The audience will find this scene hilarious, even as they watch someone die on stage.

> [stabs himself]
> Thus die I, thus, thus, thus.
> Now am I dead,
> Now am I fled;
> My soul is in the sky:
> Tongue, lose thy light;
> Moon take thy flight:
> [exit Moonshine]
> Now die, die, die, die, die.
> [dies]
>
> (act 5 scene 1)

While scholars point to these two works as potential sources for Shakespeare's play, the fairies, including Oberon, Titania, and the enduring character of Puck, all seem to leap from his own imagination.

In the next chapter, we'll take a look at how other writers and producers have used elements of *A Midsummer Night's Dream* to create new work for a modern world.

Shakespeare used several different sources to make a new tapestry out of work that his audiences would have found familiar.

KEY QUESTIONS

- How does Shakespeare show that the state of being in love is like a dream?

- Why does Shakespeare include fairies in his story about four humans? What role do the fairies play in the human world?

- How does the play-within-the-play affect the play as a whole?

COMPARE AND CONTRAST

When Shakespeare borrowed plot points and characters from other works of literature, he was acknowledging a long literary tradition. How did he change the work he borrowed to fit his own?

• **Read Ovid's section about Pyramus and Thisbe.** You can find it here.

 🔍 Ovid Metamorphoses Pyramus Thisbe

• **What do you notice about the language?** Are the characters different? What about the descriptions?

• **Read the play as presented by the tradesmen at the end of *A Midsummer Night's Dream*.** You can find it here.

 🔍 Midsummer Night's Dream act 5 scene 1

• **Investigate the similarities between the two texts.** What is the same about them? Think about the differences as well. Consider the following points and list both the similarities and differences for each.

- characters
- action
- plot
- imagery
- description

> To investigate more, write up your findings in an essay. For each point above, describe the similarities and differences in one paragraph. Add an introduction and a conclusion to the beginning and end of your essay.

Chapter Eight ▷

The Midsummer Night Magic of Today

How does a play about fairies and confusing relationships appeal to contemporary audiences?

While most people don't believe in fairies anymore, relationships can still be confusing and it's always tempting to blame mischief on creatures that don't actually exist.

It might seem difficult for people today to connect with stories about fairies and magical mischief. Young children tend to appreciate these kinds of stories, but once people reach a certain age, their tastes in magic often veer toward wizards such as Harry Potter or science fiction stories such as *Star Wars*. Magic that happens in forests and involves tiny flying creatures tends to be less interesting.

But *A Midsummer Night's Dream* has survived for centuries as a foundation for contemporary movies and books. What might be attractive about these stories for teenagers and adults?

A DREAMY MIDSUMMER MOVIE

Some writers and moviemakers use Shakespeare as source material to produce a movie that is a very close reflection of the play it's based on. A movie called *William Shakespeare's A Midsummer Night's Dream*, made in 1999, uses this technique to bring the dreamy play to the large screen and to a large audience.

Instead of ancient Greece providing the setting, an Italian village in the early twentieth century provides the backdrop to the story of four human lovers and their fateful nights in the forest. Other than the setting, little is changed.

The same plot applies—Hermia and Lysander are in love; Hermia's father, Egeus, wants her to marry Demetrius, who also loves Hermia; Helena is deeply in love with Demetrius. Duke Theseus orders Hermia to marry the man her father has chosen for her—Demetrius—or else suffer death or remain single forever.

The movie version of the play suggests an interesting interpretation of the duke's role in this scene. Remember, the duke is looking forward to getting married in a few days. In the movie, his fiancee, Hippolyta, witnesses his exchange with Ergeus and Hermia, and obviously disapproves of his decision, even though he is only following the law.

In the early 1900s, women were still considered the property of their fathers until marriage and of their husbands after, but early hints of the women's rights movement can be discerned from Hippolyta's expression. "What kind of man am I marrying?" she seems to be asking herself.

The four humans run off into the woods and the fairy people produce the magical love potion. Puck meddles in the lives of humans and mixes everyone up.

> Just as in Shakespeare's play, all of the lovers end up with the person they are meant to be with—Helena with Demetrius and Hermia with Lysander.

FOLIO FACT

Most of the movies we've looked at in this book vary widely from the original play. The structure, characters, and some of the themes have stayed constant, but the look of the movie is very different from Shakespeare's play. *The Lion King* might not even be recognizable as *Hamlet*, unless you knew the story.

A MIDSUMMER NIGHT'S DREAM

MPAA has rated this movie PG-13 for some sexual content.

RIDING BIKES

Bicycles play a large role in the movie version of *A Midsummer Night's Dream*. Many of the human characters ride them around the town and into the forest. Susan B. Anthony, a leader of the women's suffrage movement, said, "Let me tell you what I think of bicycling. I think it has done more to emancipate women than anything else in the world. It gives women a feeling of freedom and self-reliance. I stand and rejoice every time I see a woman ride by on a wheel . . . the picture of free, untrammeled womanhood."

Many people believe that bicycles gave women the independence they wanted and the freedom they needed to begin fighting seriously for their right to vote and make their own decisions. Why do you think the producers of the movie gave bicycles to the women to ride around the Italian countryside?

While the movie follows the play nearly exactly, setting the scene in the early twentieth century allows the writers and producers to explore different themes, including the roles of men and women. Do you think men and women are equal? Do you think they should be treated the same, paid the same, and allowed to do all the same things? In Shakespeare's time, this was not a popular viewpoint. Helena points this out when she says the following to Demetrius, while she follows him through the woods.

> Ay, in the temple, in the town, the field,
> You do me mischief. Fie, Demetrius!
> Your wrongs do set a scandal on my sex:
> We cannot fight for love, as men may do;
> We should be wood and were not made to woo.

(act 2 scene 1)

What is she saying about men and women? In the movie, Helena delivers this line in anger and frustration, as if she wishes for the freedom to pursue whatever she wants.

[
The movie version brings this theme of equality among men and women into sharp relief.
]

Even though Shakespeare lived in a time when women weren't considered equal to men, many of his female characters were strong, including Hippolyta. Do you think he would have approved of a feminist reading of his plays? Why or why not?

MAGICAL BOOKS

Just as Celia Rees did in her novel based on *Twelfth Night*, Susan Cooper fleshes out the character of William Shakespeare in her novel, *King of Shadows*.

In *King of Shadows*, Nat Fields is a young actor who's had the great pleasure of being chosen as part of the Boy's Company, an acting group consisting of kids from all over the United States. The year is 1999 and the Boy's Company is scheduled to perform *A Midsummer's Night Dream* at the newly opened Globe Theatre in London.

For Nat, this opportunity is more than just a chance to hone his acting skills and work with the greatest of talents. Nat is also looking for an escape from the loss he still feels acutely. Both of his parents are dead and he lives with his Aunt Jane. He looks forward to being somewhere with strangers.

At first, everything is wonderful. He loves England, he appreciates working with the talented boys, and he respects the demanding but gruff director. Everything is going well until one night he goes to sleep with a fever and wakes up 400 years in the past.

Cooper offers her readers tactile and visual cues to make Nat's experience of sixteenth-century England vibrant and immersive.

> Even before six in the morning, the street was filled with people bustling about, carrying huge bundles, selling fruit or pastries or pamphlets from trays slung around their necks, dodging to avoid men or horses. Carts clattered over the cobbles, creaking, rocking, splashing up muck sometimes from the stinking ditches into which Harry and everyone else had emptied their waste.

CHOOSING A FORMAT

When authors think about writing a book based on an older piece of work, they have a lot of decisions to make. Will they choose one character and write a new story about that person? Will they set the plot in a different time and place, as Walter Dean Myers did with *Street Love*, his book about a modern-day *Romeo and Juliet*? Or will they make Shakespeare himself a character and set him among the characters of his own plays, as Celia Rees did in *A Fool's Girl*?

FOLIO FACT

Readers get a glimpse of what it was really like in Shakespeare's time. It was messy, noisy, smelly, and fun.

Nat discovers that he's an apprentice working and performing with Lord Chamberlain's Men at the Globe Theatre of 1599. Soon, he has the pleasure of meeting Shakespeare. The company is hard at work on a production of *A Midsummer Night's Dream,* which Queen Elizabeth has expressed an interest in coming to see.

Luckily, Nat has the same part in the 1599 play as he did in the 1999 play—Puck. His acting and acrobatics are met with great approval, especially by Shakespeare himself, who is playing Oberon. Shakespeare and Nat become friends.

Shakespeare learns about Nat's history and discovers how much Nat misses his parents, especially his father. He offers Nat a sonnet he wrote about love that he hopes will help Nat deal with his enormous loss. The sonnet Shakespeare gives to Nat exists in real life as "Sonnet 116."

> Let me not to the marriage of true minds
> Admit impediments. Love is not love
> Which alters when it alteration finds,
> Or bends with the remover to remove:
> O no! it is an ever-fixed mark
> That looks on tempests and is never shaken;
> It is the star to every wandering bark,
> Whose worth's unknown, although his height
> be taken.
> Love's not Time's fool, though rosy lips and cheeks
> Within his bending sickle's compass come:
> Love alters not with his brief hours and weeks,
> But bears it out even to the edge of doom.
> If this be error and upon me proved,
> I never writ, nor no man ever loved.

At the opening of the play, the bond between Nat and Shakespeare is evident in the scenes they share. They easily slip into a father-son role that lasts beyond the stage. The play is a success, but Nat is terrified at the thought of losing his relationship with Shakespeare.

When Nat returns to 1999, he has trouble believing that everything that happened to him in 1599 actually happened. He wonders if it was a dream. When his friend finds a tiny bit of paint left over from Nat's 1599 costume, he's relieved to know it was real. "Suddenly sunlight was filling the world, suddenly I was trying not to grin, not to shout. It wasn't a dream, it wasn't a dream, it wasn't a dream . . . ."

Dreams are important in Shakespeare's original play, too. The four lovers are rooted in the reality of their situation until they all fall asleep and wake up in a dreamier reality, where their love for specific people no longer feels real. When they wake again, they decide that everything that happened was a dream. Demetrius says, "Why, then, we are awake: let's follow him / And by the way let us recount our dreams."

Write down what you think each word means: **women's rights movement**, **suffrage**, **feminist**, **acute**, and **immersive**.

Compare your definitions with those of your friends or classmates. Did you all come up with the same meanings? Turn to the text and glossary if you need help.

KEY QUESTIONS

• Have you ever seen one of Shakespeare's plays performed? What did you think?

• How much freedom do you think a writer or producer has in reinterpreting classic literature? Are there any rules they should follow?

Cooper uses Puck's ending speech for many of the same reasons Shakespeare used it. The speech is a reminder to the audience that watching and appreciating a play (or novel) requires a suspension of disbelief, and that there is magic in literature to make people feel things that aren't really happening, as in a dream.

> That you have but slumber'd here
> While these visions did appear.
> And this weak and idle theme,
> No more yielding but a dream . . . .
>
> (act 5 scene 1)

You've learned about four of Shakespeare's plays and different ways that contemporary writers, artists, and musicians have interpreted these plays and been inspired to create new works.

> You've explored some of the themes that these plays contain, and looked at the language Shakespeare used to make his audience understand what his plays were about.

Though there is no evidence that Shakespeare traveled widely and his life of 54 years was a relatively short one, the number of things he seemed to be interested in, as shown by what he wrote about, was great. Maybe that is why, today, 400 years after his death, we still read his work and use it as inspiration to create our own works.

YOUR TURN

Which of the plays discussed in this book did you find the most interesting? Are you inspired by any of the plots or themes you've learned about? Use this interest to come up with something new.

- **Who was your favorite character in *Romeo and Juliet*?** Provide that character with an interesting backstory. What was their childhood like? Did they ever have a favorite pet? Write a story about a time they were scared of something. How does Shakespeare's play influence your own work?

- **Is there anything in *Hamlet* that you wish had happened differently?** Write a play with the same characters that turns out differently. What happens instead of the fight scene at the end? Who survives? Why do they survive? How different can you make the story and have it still be recognizable as *Hamlet*?

- **Can you rewrite *Twelfth Night* so that it isn't a comedy?** What would have to happen to make it a tragedy? Try to change the plot to cause the characters grief and heartbreak instead of happiness.

- **What kind of play would *A Midsummer Night's Dream* be if it had one more act in it?** What might happen the day after the triple wedding? Continue Shakespeare's tale for slightly longer than he intended and see what you end up with! What happens?

> To investigate more, explore a story that combines the characters from all four plays into one new piece of work. How do the different characters interact with each other? What new things might they discover about themselves?

ACT OUT!

Shakespeare probably never meant for people to read his plays quietly to themselves. Most of his plays weren't even published in book format during his lifetime. Instead, he wrote his works to be performed on the stage and enjoyed by everyone who paid their pennies. The experience of seeing a Shakespeare play performed can be vastly different from reading it. To gain an even greater understanding of the lines, you can perform the play yourself.

SHAKESPEARE'S GLOBE

The Globe Theatre was rebuilt in 1997 in London according to research and archaeological excavations done on the original theater. The new building stands just a few hundred yards from the original site and is a faithful reproduction of that building, except for modern-day requirements according to safety regulations. You can see a walking tour of the theater here.

 PS Read more about the history of the new Globe Theatre here.

 Globe Theatre walking tour video · Shakespeare's Globe history

- **With a group of friends, decide which play you will perform a scene from.** You Shakespeare MIT can read all of each of Shakespeare's plays at this website.

Here are some scenes that include several players.

- *Midsummer Night's Dream*, act 2 scene 1
- *Hamlet*, act 3 scene 2
- *Twelfth Night*, act 1 scene 4
- *Romeo and Juliet*, act 3 scene 2

- **Assign roles to each person.** Some people might need to play more than one role, as long as the parts aren't on the stage at the same time.

- **Each person should read through their own parts and get a feel for the language.** Try reading the parts out loud in a room by yourself to work on pronunciation and rhythm.

- **Find clothing you can use that resembles what characters might have worn.** Are there any sword fights? Do you need to find props and choreograph any fighting scenes?

- **Decide on a stage area and rehearse the scene as a group.** Figure out where to enter and exit. Everyone should be aware of their cues and enter the scene when they hear their cue. This will take some practice!

To investigate more, perform your scene for an audience of other students or family members. What do you learn from the play when you perform it that you didn't learn just by reading it? Are you able to memorize any of your lines? What happens to the language as you get more and more familiar with it. Does it become easier to understand?

GLOSSARY

absurd: wildly unreasonable, illogical, or inappropriate.

accessible: able to be understood or entered.

accusatory: suggesting that one believes a person has done something wrong.

acknowledge: to accept or admit the existence of.

acute: having a clear understanding.

acutely: intensely.

alderman: a member of the governing body of a town.

allure: something that is tempting and attractive.

amass: to gather together or accumulate.

animosity: strong hostility.

anticipation: expectation or prediction.

apocalypse: an event involving destruction or damage on a catastrophic scale.

apprentice: someone who agrees to work for a certain amount of time for a craftsman or professional in return for being taught a trade.

archaeology: the scientific study of the remains of past human life and activities.

architecture: the style or look of a building.

artifact: an object made by people from past cultures, including tools, pottery, and jewelry.

ascend: to climb, to move upward.

authentic: genuine or real.

avenge: to punish someone who has wronged you or someone close to you.

banish: to send someone away from a country or place as an official punishment.

baptize: to make a person into a member of a group, often a church, by dipping the person into water or sprinkling water on their head.

bequeath: to hand down after death.

bloodletting: removing a person's blood as a medical treatment.

burden: a heavy load.

burgess: a member of the governing body of a town.

capacity: the maximum amount something can hold.

chamberlain: a town treasurer.

changeling: a child believed to have been secretly switched with a fairy child.

character: a person in a play, novel, or debate.

charity: an organization that helps people in need.

choreograph: to arrange or direct a dance, play, or interaction.

clan: a group of families that are related.

clarity: the quality of being clear.

collaborate: to work together.

colony: a country or area that is under the part or full political control of another country.

comedy: a drama of light and amusing characters and typically with a happy ending.

comic relief: the inclusion of a funny character or scene in an otherwise serious work.

concoction: a mixture of different ingredients.

confide: to tell a secret.

conniving: deceiving, shrewd.

conspiracy: a secret plan among two or more people to do something wrong or harmful.

constable: a public officer responsible for certain duties.

construe: to understand the meaning and intent of a sentence or larger piece of work.

contemporary: existing at the same time as something else.

controversy: an argument that involves many people who strongly disagree.

couplet: two lines of poetry that usually rhyme.

cue: a signal.

culture: the beliefs and way of life of a group of people, which can include religion, language, art, clothing, food, holidays, and more.

debt: an amount of money or something else that is owed.

desolation: a state of emptiness or misery.

destiny: events that will happen in the future.

dichotomy: a division into two opposite groups.

disbelief: the feeling that something isn't true or real.

discern: to recognize or understand something.

discrimination: the unfair treatment of a person or a group of people because of their identity.

dissipate: to scatter in different directions.

distilment: a purification of something, for example, poison.

divergent: different or developing in different directions.

dominate: to have a strong influence.

dynamic: active or changing, showing a lot of energy or motion.

dystopia: an imagined place where everything is bad.

ego: a person's sense of self-esteem or self-importance.

element: a part of something.

Elizabethan Age: the age in English history defined by the reign of Queen Elizabeth I (1558–1603). Often considered to be a golden age with many achievements and much prosperity.

emoji: a small digital image or icon used to express an idea in electronic communication.

emotion: a strong feeling about something or somebody.

enclosure: an area that is sealed off with a barrier.

enduring: long lasting.

enmity: a feeling of hostility or hatred.

entourage: a group of attendants or associates.

Eustachian tube: a tube leading from the side of the throat to the inner ear.

exhort: to strongly encourage someone to do something.

exile: when someone is barred from their home or country.

GLOSSARY

fate: the development of events beyond a person's control. The opposite of free will.

feisty: lively, determined, and curious.

feminist: a person who believes men and women should have equal rights and opportunities.

feud: a fight between two families that lasts for generations.

First Folio: the first collection of Shakespeare's plays to be published.

foil: to interrupt.

foreshadowing: a warning of a future event.

free verse: a poem that doesn't rhyme or follow a regular structure.

free will: the belief that people make choices to guide their own lives. The opposite of fate.

fruition: when an idea becomes reality.

garter: an elastic band worn around the leg to hold up a stocking.

gender: male or female.

glover: someone who makes or sells gloves.

groundling: a spectator in the cheap part of a theater.

harbor: to keep safe.

havoc: widespread destruction.

high bailiff: a town officer nominated by the king.

hilarity: extreme amusement and laughing.

humanity: the quality of being human.

iambic pentameter: a kind of poetry in which an unstressed syllable is followed by a stressed syllable, with five of these on one line.

icon: a widely recognized symbol of a certain time, or a person or thing that grows to represent a larger idea.

imagery: the use of language to represent images or ideas.

immersive: to deeply and completely engage.

immune system: the network of cells in your body that fights invading cells.

impersonate: to pretend to be another person.

indecency: bad behavior.

indecision: the inability to make a decision.

inevitable: unavoidable.

influence: to have an affect on the character, development, or outcome of something.

innovator: a person who introduces new ideas or methods.

inspiring: to make someone want to do or create something.

insurmountable: unable to be done or conquered.

integration: that act of bringing things together.

interpret: to think about something and explain it.

interracial: involving different races.

interspersed: scattered throughout.

intimidating: making another person fearful with threats or other shows of power.

jurisdiction: the official power to make legal decisions and judgments.

lament: a passionate expression of grief or sorrow.

leprous: infected with leprosy, an infectious disease.

literary: having to do with reading, writing, and literature.

literary device: a technique a writer uses to produce a certain effect in their writing.

literature: written work such as poems, plays, and novels.

loin: the part of the body on both sides of the lower spine.

lovelorn: unhappy because of love that isn't returned.

lyrical: having a light, melodic quality.

maxim: a short statement expressing a general truth or rule.

metafiction: fiction in which the author references the work as an object of literature.

metaphor: using a word or phrase that normally means one thing to mean something else, such as "a sea of trouble."

money-lending: one who lends money as a business.

morality: a system of values and principles concerned with what is right and what is wrong.

morals: a person's standards of behavior or belief.

mortality: the condition of being subject to death.

motif: an idea, pattern, image, or theme that is used in many works of art.

motto: a short phrase that describes a group's beliefs.

mourning: to show sadness about someone's death.

municipal: having to do with a city's activities or management.

muse: a source of inspiration for creative work.

mutiny: a revolt or rebellion against authority.

nobility: a person of high rank or birth.

ominous: threatening, giving the impression that something bad is going to happen.

original: something that serves as a model for imitations or copies.

parallel: behaving similarly to something else.

paralyzing: to cause someone to not be able to move or act.

passive: receiving, enduring, or submitting without resistance.

patronage: the support of an artist by someone who is wealthy.

persona: the aspect of someone's character that is presented to or perceived by others.

pickpocket: someone who steals money or other valuables from other people's pockets or bags.

pine: to long for.

piteous: deserving of feelings of sympathy and pity.

plagiarize: to steal and pass off the ideas or words of another as one's own.

plague: a contagious disease characterized by fever and delirium, or not knowing what's going on around you.

GLOSSARY

playwright: a person who writes plays.

plot: the main pattern of events in a literary work.

popular culture: books, movies, music, and other forms of art that appear to large populations of people.

portray: to describe someone or something in a particular way.

poultice: a soft, usually heated substance that is spread on cloth and then placed on the skin to heal a sore or reduce pain.

predetermine: to establish or decide in advance.

prejudice: opinion that is not based on reason or experience but on misconceptions and early judgments.

problematic: presenting a problem.

profane: to treat something sacred with abuse, irreverence, or contempt.

profit: the money made by a business after paying all the costs of the business.

prohibit: to make illegal.

prologue: an introduction to a literary work.

prominent: important.

prop: an object used in a play.

prosperity: a state of success, wealth, or comfort.

purport: to claim to be something false.

rampant: wild and out of control.

rapier: a thin, sharp sword.

reconcile: to cause people or groups to become friendly again after an argument.

reinterpretation: to look at something in a different way.

relevant: something that matters to your experience.

rendition: a performance or interpretation.

resolution: a firm decision to do or not do something.

resonate: to have particular meaning or importance.

resources: something a country has that supports its wealth, such as oil, water, food, money, and land.

respective: belonging separately to each of several people.

retention: the continued possession of something.

revelry: a party.

rhythm: a regular repeated pattern of sound.

riotous: wild and uncontrolled behavior.

ritual: an action performed in a certain way, often as part of a religion.

rubble: broken fragments.

sanitation: conditions relating to public health and cleanliness.

scaffolding: a temporary structure a person uses to reach high above the floor or ground, or the structure of a piece of literature.

sexism: prejudice, stereotyping, or discrimination on the basis of gender.

signature role: a role that an actor is best known for.

simile: a figure of speech that compares two different things using the words "like" or "as."

sleeping draught: a drink that has ingredients to put a person to sleep.

social commentary: using literature and other media to provide commentary on issues in a society.

society: a group of people with shared laws, traditions, and values.

socioeconomic: the interaction of social and economic factors.

soliloquy: when a character speaks their thoughts aloud when they are alone.

sonnet: a poem that usually has 14 lines written in iambic pentameter.

spectrum: the whole range of ideas, qualities, and situations.

star-crossed: doomed to end in tragedy.

stereotype: to make a judgment about a group of individuals.

strife: anger or bitter disagreement.

stymied: discouraged or defeated.

subplot: a plot that is related to but less important than the main plot of a story.

suffrage: the right to vote.

suitor: someone who pursues a relationship with someone else.

surfeiting: consuming something to excess, such as eating too much food.

suspension of disbelief: a willingness to believe the unbelievable.

tapestry: a thick embroidered curtain.

tenuous: very weak, shaky.

thatch: straw, leaves, or any similar material used for making a roof.

theme: a central, recurring idea or concept.

timeless: not affected by the passage of time.

toil: to work.

tone: the general character of a piece of writing.

torment: to anger or annoy.

tradesmen: a skilled worker, such as a stonecutter.

tragedy: a drama that portrays a disastrous, often fatal, series of events.

trauma: a deeply distressing or disturbing experience.

tributary: a river or stream that flows into a larger lake or river.

trope: a significant, recurring theme.

uncertainty: the feeling of being unsure, not confident.

undermine: to damage or weaken.

undertone: an underlying quality or feeling.

vandal: a person who deliberately destroys or damages public or private property.

vengeance: punishment inflicted in retaliation for wrongdoing.

verse: writing arranged with a metrical rhythm, typically having a rhyme.

vibrant: full of energy and enthusiasm.

visionary: able to anticipate the future and see ways of doing things before many others do.

whitawer: someone who works with soft leather.

women's rights movement: a movement to secure equal rights for women.

RESOURCES

BOOKS

The Shakespeare Book. DK Publishers. New York, NY. 2015

Essential Shakespeare Handbook. Dunton-Downer, Leslie, and Riding, Alan. DK Publishers. New York, NY. 2004

Shakespeare: The World as Stage. Bryson, Bill. Harper Perennial. New York, NY. 2007

Will's Words: How William Shakespeare Changed the Way You Talk. Sutcliffe, Jane. Charlesbridge. Watertown, MA. 2016

A Shakespearean Theater. Morley, Jacqueline. Scribo. Brighton, England. 2015

Novels mentioned in this book

Street Love. Myers, Walter Dean. Harper Teen. New York, NY. 2007

Romiette and Julio. Draper, Sharon M. Simon and Shuster. New York, NY. 2001

Ophelia. Klein, Lisa. Bloomsbury USA Children's. New York, NY. 2006

The Wednesday Wars. Schmidt, Gary D. HMH Books for Young Readers. New York, NY. 2009

Fool's Girl. Rees, Celia. Bloomsbury UK. London, England. 2011

King of Shadows. Cooper, Susan. Margaret K. McElderry Books. New York, NY. 2001

WEBSITES

Folger Shakespeare Library offers classroom resources, materials, primary sources, and information about performances.
folger.edu

Shakespeare's Globe contains digital tours, learning resources, and plenty of learning opportunities.
shakespearesglobe.com

PBS's "In Search of Shakespeare" has games, videos, and lots of information about Shakespeare's life.
pbs.org/shakespeare

The Shakespeare Society offers texts, play information, classes, and much more.
shakespearesociety.org

You can find the complete works of Shakespeare for free, online.
shakespeare.mit.edu

Looking for a Shakespeare festival near you?
Check the Shakespeare Resource Center
and the Global Electronic Shakespeare Conference.
bardweb.net/theatres.html
shaksper.net/scholarly-resources/shakespeare-festivals-and-plays

QR CODE GLOSSARY

Page 6: shakespeare.org.uk/visit-the-houses/anne-hathaways-cottage-amp-gardens.html

Page 12: absoluteshakespeare.com/trivia/timeline/timeline.htm

Page 12: onedayhistory.com

Page 12: onthisday.com

Page 28: cdc.gov/phpr/documents/zombie_gn_final.pdf

Page 33: youtube.com/watch?v=8xg3vE8Ie_E

Page 34: youtube.com/watch?v=mxfjSnMN88U

Page 45: youtube.com/watch?v=UbxMhvcxJJc

Page 46: youtube.com/watch?v=RF0k4qV1I1Y

Page 49: shakespeare.mit.edu/hamlet/hamlet.3.1.html

Page 58: last.fm/music/MC+Lars/_/Hey+There+Ophelia

Page 73: shakespeare.mit.edu/twelfth_night

Page 82: youtube.com/watch?v=OJQtc7oZxRg

Page 96: ovid.lib.virginia.edu/trans/Metamorph4.htm#478205190

Page 96: shakespeare.mit.edu/midsummer/midsummer.5.1.html

Page 102: youtube.com/watch?v=I7_m1om82o4

Page 106: shakespeare.mit.edu

Page 106: youtube.com/watch?v=m3VGa6Fp3zI

Page 106: shakespearesglobe.com/about-us/history-of-the-globe

ACTIVITY ANSWERS

Page 24

a) fever

b) plague

d) wounds

e) wounds

f) earache

g) mental health problems

i) kidney stones

j) fever

l) malaria

n) migraine

o) leprosy

q) dysentery

r) jaundice

INDEX

INDEX

poetry, ix, 9–10, 16–17, 33–34, 102
Polonius (character), 40, 41–42, 45, 46, 58
Puck (character), 88, 90–91, 93, 95, 99, 102, 104
Pumbaa (character), 53
Pyramus (character), 92, 95

R

R (character), 2, 26–29
Rafiki (character), 54
readings of Shakespearean works, 8–11, 73
revenge/vengeance
 in *Hamlet* and related stories, 40, 42–43, 44, 45–46, 48, 52, 55
 in *Twelfth Night* contemporary stories, 81, 82–83
Romeo (character), 2–3, 16–20, 22, 27–28
Romeo and Juliet
 contemporary references to, 2–3, 10, 26–36, 83, 101
 date of writing of, vii
 fate *vs.* free will in, 20–21
 inspirations for, 21–23, 35
 length of, 15
 plot or story of, 14, 15–20
"Romeo & Juliet" (Dire Straits), 34
Romiette and Julio (Draper), 34–35
Rosaline (character), 16
Rosencrantz (character), 40–41, 42, 55
Rosencrantz and Guildenstern Are Dead (Stoppard), 55

S

Scar (character), 53–54
Sebastian (character), 65, 67–70, 73, 77, 78, 82
self-care and selfishness, 45–46, 58
A Series of Unfortunate Events (Snicket), 31
sexism, 80–81. *See also* gender issues

Shakespeare, Hamnet, vi, vii, 5, 38, 84
Shakespeare, Judith, vi, 5
Shakespeare, Susanna, vi, 5
Shakespeare, William
 contemporary story references to, 31, 82, 83, 84, 101, 102–103
 early years and family history of, vi–ix, 3–5, 6, 8, 38, 84
 Hamlet by, viii, 7, 8, 15, 38–49, 52–61, 83
 A Midsummer Night's Dream by, vii, 83, 88–96, 98–107
 readings of works of, 8–11, 73
 Romeo and Juliet by, vii, 2–3, 10, 14–24, 26–36, 83, 101
 sonnets by, ix, 9–10, 16–17, 102
 stage performances of works of, vii, viii, 6–8, 32, 47, 101–102, 106–107
 timeline of, vi–ix, 12
 Twelfth Night by, viii, 64–73, 76–85, 101
She's the Man (movie), 77–81
Simba (character), 53–55
social commentary, 71
songs or music, 26, 33–34, 36, 58, 65, 82, 102
sonnets, ix, 9–10, 16–17, 102
stage performances, vii, viii, 6–8, 32, 47, 101–102, 106–107
Stephano (character), 82
A Story Newly Found of Two Noble Lovers (da Porto), 22
Stratford-upon-Avon, viii, ix, 4, 5, 7, 84
Street Love (Myers), 32–34, 101

T

theater performances. *See* stage performances
Theseus, Duke (character), 89, 90, 92, 94, 99
Thisbe (character), 92, 95
timeline, vi–ix, 12
Timon (character), 53

Titania, Queen (character), 90–91, 95
Toby, Sir (character), 67, 68, 69, 71
tragedy, 18–19, 3?, 38
"The Tragicall History of Romeus and Juliet" (Brooke), 21–22, 23, 35
Twelfth Night
 contemporary references to, 76–85, 101
 date of writing of, viii
 inspirations for/origins of, 72
 plot or story of, 64, 65–71, 73, 76
 themes in, 71
 title of, 71
Tybalt (character), 17, 18–19, 22

U

Ur-Hamlet (Kyd), 48

V

Viola/male counterpart (character), 64, 65–70, 73, 77–81, 80, 82
violence
 in *Hamlet* and related stories, 39–47, 52
 in *Romeo and Juliet* and related stories, 15, 16, 18–20, 27, 30, 34
 in *Twelfth Night,* 69
Violetta (character), 82–83
Vita Amlethi (Saxo Grammaticus), 48

W

Warm Bodies (movie), 2–3, 10, 26–29
We Are In a Book (Williams), 31
"The Wedding March" (Mendelssohn), 102
The Wednesday Wars (Schmidt), 58–60
West Side Story (play/movie), 32
William Shakespeare's A Midsummer Night's Dream (movie), 98–100

Y

Yorick (character), 44, 45, 83